The Law and Identity Reader

Cultivating Understanding, Agency, and Advocacy

FIRST EDITION

Edited by
Jason Leggett and Helen-Margaret Nasser

Kingsborough Community College

Bassim Hamadeh, CEO and Publisher
Claire Benson, Acquisitions Editor
Sean Adams, Project Editor
Berenice Quirino, Associate Production Editor
Jess Estrella, Senior Graphic Designer
Alisa Munoz, Licensing Associate
Don Kesner, Interior Designer
Kassie Graves, Director of Acquisitions and Sales
Jamie Giganti, Senior Managing Editor

Cover: Photograph by Jing Wen.

Printed in the United States of America.

ISBN: 978-1-5165-0913-3 (pbk) / 978-1-5165-0914-0 (br)

HUMAN RIGHTS ARE
WOMEN'S
LGBTQ+
NATIVE
BLACK
LATINX
IMMIGRANT
REFUGEE
MUSLIM
ALL RELIGION
HOMELESS
DISABILITY
SURVIVOR
VETERAN
ELDER
CHILD
STUDENT
AMERICAN RIGHTS.

THE LAW AND IDENTITY READER

Cultivating Understanding, Agency, and Advocacy

Edited by Jason Leggett and Helen-Margaret Nasser

The Law and Identity Reader

Cultivating Understanding, Agency, and Advocacy

FIRST EDITION

CONTENTS

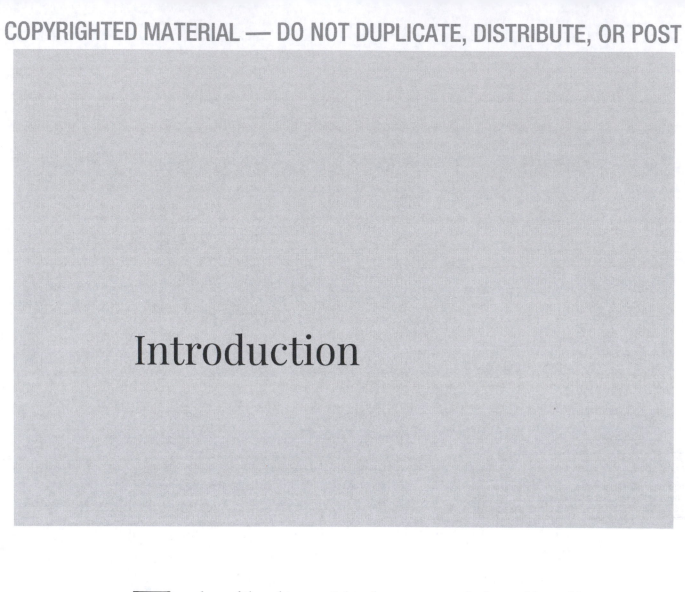

Introduction

Freedom of thought, essential to democracy, can be best evidenced in education through the practice of it in dialogue with others. We have designed this anthology as an extension of that dialogue about how civic change is possible and what challenges need to be overcome for everyone to be included in these changes. We began the process of curriculum redesign in the fall of 2012 as relative outsiders to higher education. Although both of us had been active in civic learning and democratic engagement in a variety of informal educational settings, we had not yet encountered the many challenges that confront formal educators in assessing both civic outcomes and understanding of course content. This anthology represents the culmination of our efforts as it relates to civic teaching and learning. What we found over this four-year intensive study was that motivation matters, particularly when confronting big questions in democracy and modern challenges throughout the world. This text approaches motivation through a culturally responsive selection of readings and provides a framework to guide learners through the process. We choose to categorize these generative themes as civic identity, agency, and advocacy.

We hope that learners may move more fluidly through this reader than traditional texts, both discovering and reflecting on a variety of civic identities, but we also believe each section and reading may be isolated and understood within this framework of civic motivation no matter where learners find themselves within the larger collection at any given time. We begin with a mini chapter that introduces the workflow of the text and models what we consider to be democratic dialogue. This was a key finding in our research and is supported by social movement research (Polletta 1998); learners are better able to engage when their identity is seen through a prism of changing social structures and attitudes, not a fixed ideal. In viewing the long arc of historical processes, students are better able to make meaning of the world around them, both existing and emerging. Civic identity then contains what learners believe of themselves in relation to the readings and the larger processes they will see in reflection all around them.

Agency is often reflected in the political cartoon: Although everyone supports some change, very few are engaged with change in their own lives and environments, particularly in thick social settings. Our experience informed us that this particular form of resistance is best overcome when learners can identify the challenge they wish to confront, are able to refer to others who have successfully overcome their own challenges, and are presented the tools and resources necessary to locate allies, begin the process of naming their actions, and provide space for reflection leading to action.

Advocacy is, for us, that moment of flow when learners are able to apply their learning outside the classroom, in the real world. We do not take this challenge lightly. While we know motivating learners outside the classroom to engage with democratic issues is difficult, we believe it is a prerequisite for democratic teaching and learning in the twenty-first century. Democracy is not a spectator sport. Whether you believe the major global problems we face may be solved politically or socially, or whether you believe they cannot, each individual deserves the opportunity to decide for him- or herself. To this end, we have provided a series of structured learning opportunities designed to elicit this transformative moment in your classroom or online setting through dialogue questions, short mini-research assignments, and a reflection within each section.

Throughout the text, we maintain two foundational research methods: (1) empirical political science (or broadly, social science) research and (2) critical participatory action research. It is our goal that teachers and learners engage with this research together. We have seen a wealth of knowledge that is co-created when learners engage with one another. We have also seen a product, so to speak, that can emerge when learners take their knowledge out into their communities and the world at large. We believe that given the tools and context, learners are best able to interrogate their roles as civic researchers, learning both responsibilities and rights, as well as the problem of choice within democratic structures. In the mini chapter below, we present the general research method as it applies to the content provided. Each subsequent chapter follows the same methodology and presentation. The text is designed to flow through a twelve-week course but can also be broken down into sections using the framework provided. Thank you for considering this anthology for your course. We invite you to engage with critical civic learning to confront and explore solutions for our most pressing global challenges, and we ask that you each consider: What happens if we don't change?

Democracy Is Not a Spectator Sport

We believe civic education means first accepting a democratic community for what it is, not coercing or entrapping learners to embrace ideals held by others. Many students, particularly those who are the first in their family to go to college, are often uncommitted to a prescribed life plan. We do not believe these learners are less civically involved or aware, because another experience of civic life other than our own is more common than not. Yet some of these students have yet to fully form a civic identity necessary to grow and thrive in education and society. We believe this is a problem of the civic commons and not solely a challenge for the classroom. If a learner is unaware of the effects of a governmental-social system or a majority view of these governmental systems after leaving college, this becomes a larger problem for social relations and arguably an ethical problem for the profession of teaching.

Not all learners are unaware; some have ill-formed or partially formed civic identities, meaning they can identify so-called politics around them but misunderstand the motives of individuals and groups, as well as the dynamics of the system. While learners are not to be fixed, there should exist meaningful choice, which includes respect and shared learning outcomes for civic learning and growth. In this section, we want to elicit "captures" of action for civic learning and democratic engagement. We encourage you to consider your departmental, program, and institutional learning goals and to ask your learners as you continue through this section: How do these readings and assignments generate new knowledge about the study of constitutional law in the global civic of the twenty-first century? We also invite you to join the conversation at our website,[1] where you can find additional resources and updates on our own progress.

DEVELOPING AN INQUIRY QUESTION

Dialogue is a key component to recognizing civic identity. When we interact with others in dialogue, we embrace a point of view about a particular subject that is unique and our own. However, this process of point-of-view expression creates a larger framework of possibilities that can be both overwhelming and empowering. Knowing we are part of a larger narrative or movement helps motivate individuals and groups toward change in solidarity with others. We invite you to take some time to think about and share what each learner thinks would be a meaningful inquiry into the question of civic identity and action, to be answered at the end of this section.

Originalism, the Lesser Evil

Justice Antonin Scalia served as one of the more colorful Supreme Court justices, often provoking admiration or disdain, sometimes both. We begin the inquiry into constitutional law in the global twenty-first century by considering his interpretation of the document, of the court, and of a just society. We then provide a series of different viewpoints to make explicit the role of individual interpretation and how identity shapes this analysis. As you read through Justice Scalia's arguments in this excerpt, consider how you might approach interpreting the US Constitution.

---

1 http://imagine1civic.commons.gc.cuny.edu/

....

from

Originalism: The Lesser Evil

University of Cincinnati Law Review 57 (1989): 852–855.[2]

Justice Antonin Scalia

It may surprise the layman, but it will surely not surprise the lawyers here, to learn that originalism is not, and had perhaps never been, the sole method of constitutional exegesis. It would be hard to count on the fingers of both hands and the toes of both feet, yea, even on the hairs of one's youthful head, the opinions that have in fact been rendered not on the basis of what the Constitution originally meant, but on the basis of what the judges currently thought it desirable for it to mean. That is, I suppose, the sort of behavior Chief Justice Hughes was referring to when he said the Constitution is what the judges say it is. But in the past, nonoriginalist opinions have almost always had the decency to lie, or at least to dissemble, about what they were doing— either ignoring strong evidence of original intent that contradicted the minimal recited evidence of an original intent congenial to the court's desires, or else not discussing original intent at all, speaking in terms of broad constitutional generalities with no pretense of historical support. [...]

The principal theoretical defect of nonoriginalism, in my view, is its incompatibility with the very principle that legitimizes judicial review of constitutionality. Nothing in the text of the Constitution confers upon the courts the power to inquire into, rather than passively assume, the constitutionality of federal statutes. That power is, however, reasonably implicit because, as Marshall said in Marbury v. Madison, (1) "[i]t is emphatically the province and duty of the judicial department to say what the law is," (2) "[i]f two laws conflict with each other, the courts must decide on the operation of each," and (3) "the constitution is to be considered, in court, as a paramount law." Central to that analysis, it seems to me, is the perception that the Constitution, though it has an effect superior to other laws, is in its nature the sort of "law" that is the business of the courts – an

---

2   Justice Antonin Scalia, "Originalism: The Lesser Evil," University of Cincinnati Law Review, vol. 57, pp. 852–855. Copyright © 1989 by University of Cincinnati/Law Review. Reprinted with permission.

enactment that has a fixed meaning ascertainable through the usual devices familiar to those learned in the law. If the Constitution were not that sort of a "law," but a novel invitation to apply current societal values, what reason would there be to believe that the invitation was addressed to the courts rather than to the legislature? One simply cannot say, regarding that sort of novel enactment, that "[i] t is emphatically the province and duty of the judicial department" to determine its content. Quite to the contrary, the legislature would seem a much more appropriate expositor of social values, and its determination that a statute is compatible with the Constitution should, as in England, prevail.

[…] If the law is to make any attempt at consistency and predictability, surely there must be general agreement not only that judges reject one exegetical approach (originalism), but that they adopt another. And it is hard to discern any emerging consensus among the nonoriginalists as to what this might be. Are the "fundamental values" that replace original meaning to be derived from the philosophy of Plato, or of Locke, or Mills, or Rawls, or perhaps from the latest Gallup poll? This is not to say that originalists are in entire agreement as to what the nature of their methodology is; as I shall mention shortly, there are some significant differences. But as its name suggests, it by and large represents a coherent approach, or at least an agreed-upon point of departure. As the name "nonoriginalism" suggests (and I know no other, more precise term by which this school of exegesis can be described), it represents agreement on nothing except what is the wrong approach.

· ·

"I Am Tired of Being Labeled"

Early in our classroom discussions with students about civic identity, one learner made a passionate and compelling case against labeling and stereotypes. She explained that stereotypes are interactions that exclude, and there is no space to emerge. I had never noticed in the classroom that she struggled with this in her past, nor had I thought about generalizing as a kind of assumption about the so-called other in any communication. It was important, she emphasized, that I stepped out of the box others put me in. When Justice Scalia envisions himself in historical terms, we should understand his civic identity, whether we agree with him or not. It is important to note that antistereotype behavior must include denying the power of the labeler, the political-legal power especially, because the right for every individual to espouse her particular belief about what it means to be a human in this particular system of self-government is beyond question. How we choose to represent our civic identity in social environments is dependent on a number of overwhelming externalities, but within any given system we can see examples—narratives like Raven-Symoné's—that provide documentation of change in dialogue with another. Removing labels with another creates an exciting and imaginative world of what the civic commons can be.

Video: Oprah Winfrey Network, "Raven-Symoné: 'I'm Tired of Being Labeled,'" Copyright © 2014 by Discovery Communications. URL: https://youtu.be/QXAho8vlmAI

Miller v. California and Robert Mapplethorpe

Nowhere is the application of the U.S. Constitution to everyday life more complicated than what is and is not artistic expression. Although the U.S. Constitution makes no mention of obscenity or the limits of art expression, it does support the progress of science and useful arts. In a constitutional democratic republic, the boundaries are largely made up through public discourse and responsive legislation. Robert Mapplethorpe was accused of obscene art in several photographs that depicted sexual themes. But even simple natural objects like flowers and symbols have caused other artists, like Georgia O'Keeffe and her famous flowers, to be labeled within the same sexual-obscene paradigm. It is important to note that the artist and the viewer have been excluded from the meaning-making moment of defining the parameters of social good. This legal exclusion is the process of effective legislative effort but runs up against the claimed protections of the Constitution and the founding documents as it relates to those individuals and groups outside of the supposed majority social norm. How one views one's own civic identity must be measured against the social norms of the time and the practices of its democratic institutions.

One major philosophical truth about constitutional government is the absolute insistence on governmental restraints or limits of power. To be free from arbitrary and capricious governmental action is a basic principal of due process and one of our only defenses as individuals. Moreover, as legal scholars have pointed out, the legal order extends into the social and economic spheres. A democratic process for forbidding certain behaviors is a difficult and complex one. However, the juries in both the Mapplethorpe and a similar contemporary case involving musical group 2 Live Crew disagreed with the legislative attempts to restrict art expression in the marketplace. These examples show how civic agency can be used in a variety of civic institutions, notably in the legislative and judicial venues.

···

from

Opinion of Chief Justice Burger

Miller v. California, 413 U.S. 15. June 21, 1973.[3]

Chief Justice Burger

This much has been categorically settled by the Court, that obscene material is unprotected by the First Amendment. *Kois v. Wisconsin*, 408 U.S. 229 (1972); *United States v. Reidel*, 402 U.S. at 354; *Roth v. United States*, supra, at 485. "The First and Fourteenth Amendments have never been treated as absolutes [footnote omitted]." *Breard v. Alexandria*, 341 U.S. at 642, and cases cited. See *Times Film Corp. v. Chicago*, 365 U.S. 43, 47–50 (1961); *Joseph Burstyn, Inc. v. Wilson*, 343 U.S. at 502. We acknowledge, however, the inherent dangers of undertaking to regulate any form of expression. State statutes designed to regulate obscene materials must be carefully limited. See *Interstate Circuit, Inc. v. Dallas*, supra, at 682–685. As a result, we now confine the permissible scope of such regulation to works which depict or describe sexual conduct. That conduct must be specifically defined by the applicable state law, as written or authoritatively construed. A state offense must also be limited to works which, taken as a whole, appeal to the prurient interest in sex, which portray sexual conduct in a patently offensive way, and which, taken as a whole, do not have serious literary, artistic, political, or scientific value.

The basic guidelines for the trier of fact must be: (a) whether "the average person, applying contemporary community standards" would find that the work, taken as a whole, appeals to the prurient interest, *Kois v. Wisconsin, supra*, at 230, quoting *Roth v. United States, supra*, at 489; (b) whether the work depicts or describes, in a patently offensive way, sexual conduct specifically defined by the applicable state law; and (c) whether the work, taken as a whole, lacks serious literary, artistic, political, or scientific value. We do not adopt as a constitutional standard the "utterly without redeeming social value" test of *Memoirs v. Massachusetts*, 383 U.S. at 419; that concept has never commanded the adherence of more than three Justices at one

---

3   Chief Justice Burger, Excerpt from "Opinion of Chief Justice Burger," *Miller v. California*, Legal Information Institute, pp. 22–26. Copyright in the Public Domain.

time. *See supra* at 21. If a state law that regulates obscene material is thus limited, as written or construed, the First Amendment values applicable to the States through the Fourteenth Amendment are adequately protected by the ultimate power of appellate courts to conduct an independent review of constitutional claims when necessary. See *Kois v. Wisconsin, supra*, at 232; *Memoirs v. Massachusetts, supra*, at 459–460 (Harlan, J., dissenting); *Jacobellis v. Ohio*, 378 U.S. at 204 (Harlan, J., dissenting); *New York Times Co. v. Sullivan*, 376 U.S. 254, 284–285 (1964); *Roth v. United States, supra*, at 497–498 (Harlan, J., concurring and dissenting).

We emphasize that it is not our function to propose regulatory schemes for the States. That must await their concrete legislative efforts. It is possible, however, to give a few plain examples of what a state statute could define for regulation under part (b) of the standard announced in this opinion, *supra:*

(a) Patently offensive representations or descriptions of ultimate sexual acts, normal or perverted, actual or simulated.

(b) Patently offensive representations or descriptions of masturbation, excretory functions, and lewd exhibition of the genitals.

Sex and nudity may not be exploited without limit by films or pictures exhibited or sold in places of public accommodation any more than live sex and nudity can be exhibited or sold without limit in such public places. At a minimum, prurient, patently offensive depiction or description of sexual conduct must have serious literary, artistic, political, or scientific value to merit First Amendment protection. See *Kois v. Wisconsin, supra*, at 230–232; *Roth v. United States, supra*, at 487; *Thornhill v. Alabama*, 310 U.S. 88, 101–102 (1940). For example, medical books for the education of physicians and related personnel necessarily use graphic illustrations and descriptions of human anatomy. In resolving the inevitably sensitive questions of fact and law, we must continue to rely on the jury system, accompanied by the safeguards that judges, rules of evidence, presumption of innocence, and other protective features provide, as we do with rape, murder, and a host of other offenses against society and its individual members.

....

DISCUSSION QUESTIONS

1. How does the process of labeling help explain the difficulties people have in expressing their interpretation of constitutional rights?
2. How do you think Robert Mapplethorpe re-formed his civic identity when he was accused of producing criminally obscene photographic art?
3. What expectations do you have of the Supreme Court to safeguard your constitutional rights and identity?

Scott v. Sandford: In Reflection

When we consider what civic identity means in a democratic, living environment, we accept as a given the natural conditions under which we must live, including access to food and water, shelter from seasonal change, security for ourselves and loved ones, and hopefully good health. Many modern communities now take these natural conditions for granted, despite the historical fact that humans have developed complicated legal and social moral decision-making institutions to safeguard these conditions. Managing this web of bureaucracy could be a nightmare for any nonprofessional. In fact, it is a large component of what professional legal researchers, judges, lawyers, clerks, paralegals, professors, and social science writers, to name a few socio-legal occupations, do daily.

Those professionals who have a global understanding of the world are more acquainted with the decision-making processes of the elites in government and private industry. Our relation to private property as an object worth protecting is discussed in much of constitutional law, but it also serves as a starting point for legal history in western civilization as a basis for the rule of law. However, property also further differentiates our relative position to the reasonably prudent or rational citizen as each pursues his or her own concept of life, liberty, and the pursuit of happiness. The value of a human life was a commodity on which the social-economic environment was built and maintained. Slavery was an economic and social-cultural fact of life, and the law, as a rule for behavior, had no influence on those who refused to believe in human equality. Customs and habits have long been known to outlive legal codes and moral dictates. Legal ordained behavior necessarily follows action of political-social groups within a jurisdiction, often called community. Who participates is a measurement of political science and legal studies, if not a number of disciplinary and interdisciplinary studies, that can help improve public policy and our public understanding of these processes.

Read the following excerpt from *Scott v. Sandford*:

···

from

Scott v. Sandford

60 U.S. 393 (1857).[4]

Upon the whole, therefore, it is the judgment of this court that it appears by the record before us that the plaintiff in error is not a citizen of Missouri in the sense in which that word is used in the Constitution, and that the Circuit Court of the United States, for that reason, had no jurisdiction in the case, and could give no judgment in it. Its judgment for the defendant must, consequently, be reversed, and a mandate issued directing the suit to be dismissed for want of jurisdiction.

The question is simply this: can a negro whose ancestors were imported into this country and sold as slaves become a member of the political community formed and brought into existence by the Constitution of the United States, and as such become entitled to all the rights, and privileges, and immunities, guaranteed by that instrument to the citizen, one of which rights is the privilege of suing in a court of the United States in the cases specified in the Constitution?

It will be observed that the plea applies to that class of persons only whose ancestors were negroes of the African race, and imported into this country and sold and held as slaves. The only matter in issue before the court, therefore, is, whether the descendants of such slaves, when they shall be emancipated, or who are born of parents who had become free before their birth, are citizens of a State in the sense in which the word "citizen" is used in the Constitution of the United States. And this being the only matter in dispute on the pleadings, the court must be understood as speaking in this opinion of that class only, that is, of those persons who are the descendants of Africans who were imported into this country and sold as slaves.

---

4   Chief Justice Taney, Excerpt from "Scott v. Sandford, 60 U.S. 393," Legal Information Institute, pp. 403–410,454. Copyright in the Public Domain.

The situation of this population was altogether unlike that of the Indian race. The latter, it is true, formed no part of the colonial communities, and never amalgamated with them in social connections or in government. But although they were uncivilized, they were yet a free and independent people, associated together in nations or tribes and governed by their own laws. Many of these political communities were situated in territories to which the white race claimed the ultimate right of dominion. But that claim was acknowledged to be subject to the right of the Indians to occupy it as long as they thought proper, and neither the English nor colonial Governments claimed or exercised any dominion over the tribe or nation by whom it was occupied, nor claimed the right to the possession of the territory, until the tribe or nation consented to cede it. These Indian Governments were regarded and treated as foreign Governments as much so as if an ocean had separated the red man from the white, and their freedom has constantly been acknowledged, from the time of the first emigration to the English colonies to the present day, by the different Governments which succeeded each other. Treaties have been negotiated with them, and their alliance sought for in war, and the people who compose these Indian political communities have always been treated as foreigners not living under our Government. It is true that the course of events has brought the Indian tribes within the limits of the United States under subjection to the white race, and it has been found necessary, for their sake as well as our own, to regard them as in a state of pupilage, and to legislate to a certain extent over them and the territory they occupy. But they may, without doubt, like the subjects of any other foreign Government, be naturalized by the authority of Congress, and become citizens of a State, and of the United States, and if an individual should leave his nation or tribe and take up his abode among the white population, he would be entitled to all the rights and privileges which would belong to an emigrant from any other foreign people.

The words "people of the United States" and "citizens" are synonymous terms, and mean the same thing. They both describe the political body who, according to our republican institutions, form the sovereignty and who hold the power and conduct the Government through their representatives. They are what we familiarly call the "sovereign people," and every citizen is one of this people, and a constituent member of this sovereignty. The question before us is whether the class of persons described in the plea in abatement compose a portion of this people, and are considered as a subordinate [p405] and inferior class of beings who had been subjugated by the dominant race, and, whether emancipated or not, yet remained subject to their authority, and had no rights or privileges but such as those who held the power and the Government might choose to grant them.

It is not the province of the court to decide upon the justice or injustice, the policy or impolicy, of these laws. The decision of that question belonged to the political or lawmaking power, to those who formed the sovereignty and framed the Constitution. The duty of the court is to interpret the instrument they have framed with the best lights we can obtain on the subject, and to administer it as we find it, according to its true intent and meaning when it was adopted.

It is very clear, therefore, that no State can, by any act or law of its own, passed since the adoption of the Constitution, introduce a new member into the political community created by the Constitution of the United States. It cannot make him a member of this community by making him a member of its own. And, for the same reason, it cannot introduce any person or description of persons who were not intended to be embraced in this new political family which the Constitution brought into existence, but were intended to be excluded from it.

It is difficult at this day to realize the state of public opinion in relation to that unfortunate race which prevailed in the civilized and enlightened portions of the world at the time of the Declaration of Independence and when the Constitution of the United States was framed and adopted. But the public history of every European nation displays it in a manner too plain to be mistaken.

They had for more than a century before been regarded as beings of an inferior order, and altogether unfit to associate with the white race either in social or political relations, and so far inferior that they had no rights which the white man was bound to respect, and that the negro might justly and lawfully be reduced to slavery for his benefit. He was bought and sold, and treated as an ordinary article of merchandise and traffic whenever a profit could be made by it.

This opinion was at that time fixed and universal in the civilized portion of the white race. It was regarded as an axiom in morals as well as in politics which no one thought of disputing or supposed to be open to dispute, and men in every grade and position in society daily and habitually acted upon it in their private pursuits, as well as in matters of public concern, without doubting for a moment the correctness of this opinion.

And in no nation was this opinion more firmly fixed or more uniformly acted upon than by the English Government and English people. They not only seized them on the coast of Africa and sold them or held them in slavery for their own use, but they took them as ordinary articles of merchandise to every country where they could make a profit on them, and were far more extensively engaged in this commerce than any other nation in the world.

The opinion thus entertained and acted upon in England was naturally impressed upon the colonies they founded on this side of the Atlantic. And, accordingly, a negro of the African race was regarded by them as an article of property, and held, and bought and sold as such, in every one of the thirteen colonies which united in the Declaration of Independence and afterwards formed the Constitution of the United States. The slaves were more or less numerous in the different colonies as slave labor was found more or less profitable. But no one seems to have doubted the correctness of the prevailing opinion of the time.

The legislation of the different colonies furnishes positive and indisputable proof of this fact.

It begins by declaring that,

> [w]hen in the course of human events it becomes necessary for one people to dissolve the political bands which have connected them with another, and to assume among the powers of the earth the separate and equal station to which the laws of nature and nature's God entitle them, a decent respect for the opinions of mankind requires that they should declare the causes which impel them to the separation.

It then proceeds to say:

> We hold these truths to be self-evident: that all men are created equal; that they are endowed by their Creator with certain unalienable rights; that among them is life, liberty, and the pursuit of happiness; that to secure these rights, Governments are instituted, deriving their just powers from the consent of the governed.

The general words above quoted would seem to embrace the whole human family, and if they were used in a similar instrument at this day would be so understood. But it is too clear for dispute that the enslaved African race were not intended to be included, and formed no part of the people who framed and adopted this declaration, for if the language, as understood in that day, would embrace them, the conduct of the distinguished men who framed the Declaration of Independence would have been utterly and flagrantly inconsistent with the principles they asserted, and instead of the sympathy of mankind to which they so confidently appealed, they would have deserved and received universal rebuke and reprobation.

Yet the men who framed this declaration were great men—high in literary acquirements, high in their sense of honor, and incapable of asserting principles inconsistent with those on which they were acting. They perfectly understood the meaning of the language they used, and how it would be understood by others, and they knew that it would not in any part of the civilized world be supposed to embrace the negro race, which, by common consent, had been excluded from civilized Governments and the family of nations, and doomed to slavery. They spoke and acted according to the then established doctrines and principles, and in the ordinary language of the day, and no one misunderstood them. The unhappy black race were separated from the white by indelible marks, and laws long before established, and were never thought of or spoken of except as property, and when the claims of the owner or the profit of the trader were supposed to need protection.

....

In reflection:

When Dred Scott and other freed slaves were told they could not become citizens, what identity or identities do you imagine they embraced to integrate into a changing society?

Answering the Inquiry Question through Dialogue

We have provided four distinct ways of making meaning around the concept of civic identity and action. We encourage you to record and document your class responses and to be a part of a larger narrative. Feel free to join the conversation by visiting our website at http://imagine1civic.commons.gc.cuny.edu/.

We all know different identities in a small space can create conflict. There are countless examples in the news or popular culture outlets that show the hate, anger, and confusion that difference provokes. But within democratic communities, much like living ecosystems with natural biodiversity, difference promotes innovation and the sharing of cultural experiences, which creates a stronger social system. One way we approached the question of difference and identity in our work was to use critical participatory action research (CPAR) to frame these questions more inclusively.

CPAR includes codesigned research projects undertaken as critical scholarship by multigenerational collectives to interrogate conditions of social injustice through social theory with a dedicated commitment to social action. As Anisur Bahman (1985) has written, the distinctive viewpoint of PAR recognizes that the domination of masses by elites is rooted in the polarization of control not only over the means of material production but also over the means of knowledge production, including the social power to determine what is valid or useful knowledge. We believe this framework is one practical example of democratic teaching and learning. We encourage you to frame the remainder of your course time as a collective problem to be solved with action research methods. What is your collective critical inquiry question? Does it make sense to create subcommittees for related and seemingly unrelated research questions? What are the steps needed to find out more information in a reliable and organized way? How can you best share your findings in a way that is transparent and accountable? What allies do you have on and off campus that can help take the research out of the classroom and into the real world? For more resources, see the next section for an example project, and see our website for templates for action research.

SECTION TWO

Civic Agency Must Be Realized through a Confrontation of Identity with a Moving Law and Society

Once we fully realize our civic identity, we must become aware of how others perceive our civic agency. What we are able to change depends on how well we are able to work with other like-minded and different civic identities. We showed in the first section how resistance to difference can be overcome by naming problems, discussing the relevance of the co-designed learning program, and authentically embracing a dialogue around difference and civic change. However, progress for some groups is often attained at a higher cost than for others. In this section, we present six critical theories that examine how groups can bring civic identity and civic agency together for change.

INQUIRY QUESTION

In our classroom sessions, we found most learners benefited from the following inquiry. Feel free to amend these questions or come up with your own!

In two columns, compare your answers to learners around you and revisit your responses at the end of the section:

1. What groups do you belong to?
2. What groups might be able to help you practice civic agency?

Clash of the Civilizations

Samuel Huntington's *Clash of Civilizations* has long been debated for its merit and accuracy. The excerpts selected below are chosen to represent the importance of identity—how an individual identity fits, or does not fit neatly, into a national identity. Huntington begins by introducing the larger concept of civilizations and why he predicts that they will clash. As you read, consider what makes civilizations distinct from one another. As we have come to observe, identities and cultures within a civilization or country are not always uniform or homogenous. Huntington introduces the idea of "torn countries," where the population is more heterogeneous and encompasses more than one civilization within it. Huntington argues that these countries are candidates for dismemberment. When reading this, the reader may want to consider the American "melting pot" and its efficacy in accepting different cultural identities.

··

from

The Clash of Civilizations?[1]
Samuel P. Huntington

The Next Pattern of Conflict

World politics is entering a new phase, and intellectuals have not hesitated to proliferate visions of what it will be—the end of history, the return of traditional rivalries between nation states, and the decline of the nation state from the conflicting pulls of tribalism and globalism, among others. Each of these visions catches aspects of the emerging reality. Yet they all miss a crucial, indeed a central, aspect of what global politics is likely to be in the coming years.

---

[1]   Samuel Huntington, "Clash of the Civilizations," *Foreign Affairs, vol. 72, no. 3*, pp. 22–29, 42–45. Copyright © 1993 by Council on Foreign Relations, Inc. Reprinted with permission.

It is my hypothesis that the fundamental source of conflict in this new world will not be primarily ideological or primarily economic. The great divisions among humankind and the dominating source of conflict will be cultural. Nation states will remain the most powerful actors in world affairs, but the principal conflicts of global politics will occur between nations and groups of different civilizations. The clash of civilizations will dominate global politics. The fault lines between civilizations will be the battle lines of the future.

Conflict between civilizations will be the latest phase in the evolution of conflict in the modern world. For a century and a half after the emergence of the modern international system with the Peace of Westphalia, the conflicts of the Western world were largely among princes—emperors, absolute monarchs and constitutional monarchs attempting to expand their bureaucracies, their armies, their mercantilist economic strength and, most important, the territory they ruled. In the process they created nation states, and beginning with the French Revolution the principal lines of conflict were between nations rather than princes. In 1793, as R. R. Palmer put it, "The wars of kings were over; the wars of peoples had begun." This nineteenth-century pattern lasted until the end of World War I. Then, as a result of the Russian Revolution and the reaction against it, the conflict of nations yielded to the conflict of ideologies, first among communism, fascism-Nazism and liberal democracy, and then between communism and liberal democracy. During the Cold War, this latter conflict became embodied in the struggle between the two superpowers, neither of which was a nation state in the classical European sense and each of which defined its identity in terms of its ideology.

These conflicts between princes, nation states and ideologies were primarily conflicts within Western civilization, "Western civil wars," as William Lind has labeled them. This was as true of the Cold War as it was of the world wars and the earlier wars of the seventeenth, eighteenth and nineteenth centuries. With the end of the Cold War, international politics moves out of its Western phase, and its centerpiece becomes the interaction between the West and non-Western civilizations and among non-Western civilizations. In the politics of civilizations, the peoples and governments of non-Western civilizations no longer remain the objects of history as targets of Western colonialism but join the West as movers and shapers of history.

The Nature of Civilizations

During the cold war the world was divided into the First, Second and Third Worlds. Those divisions are no longer relevant. It is far more meaningful now to group countries not in terms of their political or economic systems or in terms of their level of economic development but rather in terms of their culture and civilization.

What do we mean when we talk of a civilization? A civilization is a cultural entity. Villages, regions, ethnic groups, nationalities, religious groups, all have distinct cultures at different levels of cultural heterogeneity. The culture of a village in southern Italy may be different from that of a village in northern Italy, but both will share in a common Italian culture that distinguishes them from German villages. European communities, in turn, will share cultural features that distinguish them from Arab or Chinese communities. Arabs, Chinese and Westerners, however, are not part of any broader cultural entity. They constitute civilizations. A civilization is thus the highest cultural grouping of people and the broadest level of cultural identity people have short of that which distinguishes humans from other species. It is defined both by common objective elements, such as language, history, religion, customs, institutions, and by the subjective self-identification of people. People have levels of identity: a resident of Rome may define himself with varying degrees of intensity as a Roman, an Italian, a Catholic, a Christian, a European, a Westerner. The civilization to which he belongs is the broadest level of identification with which he intensely identifies. People can and do redefine their identities and, as a result, the composition and boundaries of civilizations change.

Civilizations may involve a large number of people, as with China ("a civilization pretending to be a state," as Lucian Pye put it), or a very small number of people, such as the Anglophone Caribbean. A civilization may include several nation states, as is the case with Western, Latin American and Arab civilizations, or only one, as is the case with Japanese civilization. Civilizations obviously blend and overlap, and may include subcivilizations. Western civilization has two major variants, European and North American, and Islam has its Arab, Turkic and Malay subdivisions. Civilizations are nonetheless meaningful entities, and while the lines between them are seldom sharp, they are real. Civilizations are dynamic; they rise and fall; they divide and merge. And, as any student of history knows, civilizations disappear and are buried in the sands of time.

Westerners tend to think of nation states as the principal actors in global affairs. They have been that, however, for only a few centuries. The broader reaches of human history have been the history of civilizations. In *A Study of History*, Arnold Toynbee identified 21 major civilizations; only six of them exist in the contemporary world.

Why Civilizations Will Clash

Civilization identity will be increasingly important in the future, and the world will be shaped in large measure by the interactions among seven or eight major civilizations. These include Western, Confucian, Japanese, Islamic, Hindu, Slavic-Orthodox, Latin American and possibly African civilization. The most important conflicts of the future will occur along the cultural fault lines separating these civilizations from one another.

Why Will This Be the Case?

First, differences among civilizations are not only real; they are basic. Civilizations are differentiated from each other by history, language, culture, tradition and, most important, religion. The people of different civilizations have different views on the relations between God and man, the individual and the group, the citizen and the state, parents and children, husband and wife, as well as differing views of the relative importance of rights and responsibilities, liberty and authority, equality and hierarchy. These differences are the product of centuries. They will not soon disappear. They are far more fundamental than differences among political ideologies and political regimes. Differences do not necessarily mean conflict, and conflict does not necessarily mean violence. Over the centuries, however, differences among civilizations have generated the most prolonged and the most violent conflicts.

Second, the world is becoming a smaller place. The interactions between peoples of different civilizations are increasing; these increasing interactions intensify civilization consciousness and awareness of differences between civilizations and commonalities within civilizations. North African immigration to France generates hostility among Frenchmen and at the same time increased receptivity to immigration by "good" European Catholic Poles. Americans react far more negatively to Japanese investment than to larger investments from Canada and European countries. Similarly, as Donald Horowitz has pointed out, "An Ibo may be … an Owerri Ibo or an Onitsha Ibo in what was the

Eastern region of Nigeria. In Lagos, he is simply an Ibo. In London, he is a Nigerian. In New York, he is an African." The interactions among peoples of different civilizations enhance the civilization-consciousness of people that, in turn, invigorates differences and animosities stretching or thought to stretch back deep into history.

Third, the processes of economic modernization and social change throughout the world are separating people from longstanding local identities. They also weaken the nation state as a source of identity. In much of the world religion has moved in to fill this gap, often in the form of movements that are labeled "fundamentalist." Such movements are found in Western Christianity, Judaism, Buddhism and Hinduism, as well as in Islam. In most countries and most religions the people active in fundamentalist movements are young, college-educated, middle-class technicians, professionals and business persons. The "unsecularization of the world," George Weigel has remarked, "is one of the dominant social facts of life in the late twentieth century." The revival of religion, "la revanche de Dieu," as Gilles Kepel labeled it, provides a basis for identity and commitment that transcends national boundaries and unites civilizations.

Fourth, the growth of civilization-consciousness is enhanced by the dual role of the West. On the one hand, the West is at a peak of power. At the same time, however, and perhaps as a result, a return to the roots phenomenon is occurring among non-Western civilizations. Increasingly one hears references to trends toward a turning inward and "Asianization" in Japan, the end of the Nehru legacy and the "Hinduization" of India, the failure of Western ideas of socialism and nationalism and hence "re-Islamization" of the Middle East, and now a debate over Westernization versus Russianization in Boris Yeltsin's country. A West at the peak of its power confronts non-Wests that increasingly have the desire, the will and the resources to shape the world in non-Western ways.

In the past, the elites of non-Western societies were usually the people who were most involved with the West, had been educated at Oxford, the Sorbonne or Sandhurst, and had absorbed Western attitudes and values. At the same time, the populace in non-Western countries often remained deeply imbued with the indigenous culture. Now, however, these relationships are being reversed. A de-Westernization and indigenization of elites is occurring in many non-Western countries at the same time that Western, usually American, cultures, styles and habits become more popular among the mass of the people.

Fifth, cultural characteristics and differences are less mutable and hence less easily compromised and resolved than political and economic ones. In the former Soviet Union, communists can become democrats, the rich can become poor and the poor rich, but Russians cannot become Estonians and Azeris cannot become Armenians. In class and ideological conflicts, the key question was "Which side are you on?" and people could and did choose sides and change sides. In conflicts between civilizations, the question is "What are you?" That is a given that cannot be changed. And as we know, from Bosnia to the Caucasus to the Sudan, the wrong answer to that question can mean a bullet in the head. Even more than ethnicity, religion discriminates sharply and exclusively among people. A person can be half-French and half-Arab and simultaneously even a citizen of two countries. It is more difficult to be half-Catholic and half-Muslim.

Finally, economic regionalism is increasing. The proportions of total trade that were intraregional rose between 1980 and 1989 from 51 percent to 59 percent in Europe, 33 percent to 37 percent in East Asia, and 32 percent to 36 percent in North America. The importance of regional economic blocs is likely to continue to increase in the future. On the one hand, successful economic regionalism will reinforce civilization-consciousness. On the other hand, economic regionalism may succeed only when it is rooted in a common civilization. The European Community rests on the shared foundation of European culture and Western Christianity. The success of the North American Free Trade Area depends on the convergence now underway of Mexican, Canadian and American cultures. Japan, in contrast, faces difficulties in creating a comparable economic entity in East Asia because Japan is a society and civilization unique to itself. However strong the trade and investment links Japan may develop with other East Asian countries, its cultural differences with those countries inhibit and perhaps preclude its promoting regional economic integration like that in Europe and North America.

Common culture, in contrast, is clearly facilitating the rapid expansion of the economic relations between the People's Republic of China and Hong Kong, Taiwan, Singapore and the overseas Chinese communities in other Asian countries. With the Cold War over, cultural commonalities increasingly overcome ideological differences, and mainland China and Taiwan move closer together. If cultural commonality is a prerequisite for economic integration, the principal East Asian economic bloc of the future is likely to be centered on

China. This bloc is, in fact, already coming into existence. As Murray Weidenbaum has observed,

> Despite the current Japanese dominance of the region, the Chinese-based economy of Asia is rapidly emerging as a new epicenter for industry, commerce and finance. This strategic area contains substantial amounts of technology and manufacturing capability (Taiwan), outstanding entrepreneurial, marketing and services acumen (Hong Kong), a fine communications network (Singapore), a tremendous pool of financial capital (all three), and very large endowments of land, resources and labor (mainland China). … From Guangzhou to Singapore, from Kuala Lumpur to Manila, this influential network—often based on extensions of the traditional clans—has been described as the backbone of the East Asian economy.[2]

Culture and religion also form the basis of the Economic Cooperation Organization, which brings together ten non-Arab Muslim countries: Iran, Pakistan, Turkey, Azerbaijan, Kazakhstan, Kyrgyzstan, Turkmenistan, Tadjikistan, Uzbekistan and Afghanistan. One impetus to the revival and expansion of this organization, founded originally in the 1960s by Turkey, Pakistan and Iran, is the realization by the leaders of several of these countries that they had no chance of admission to the European Community. Similarly, Caricom, the Central American Common Market and Mercosur rest on common cultural foundations. Efforts to build a broader Caribbean-Central American economic entity bridging the Anglo-Latin divide, however, have to date failed.

As people define their identity in ethnic and religious terms, they are likely to see an "us" versus "them" relation existing between themselves and people of different ethnicity or religion. The end of ideologically defined states in Eastern Europe and the former Soviet Union permits traditional ethnic identities and animosities to come to the fore. Differences in culture and religion create differences over policy issues, ranging from human rights to immigration to trade and commerce to the environment. Geographical propinquity gives rise to

---

2   Murray Weidenbaum, *Greater China: The Next Economic Superpower?*, St. Louis: Washington University Center for the Study of American Business, Contemporary Issues. Series 57. February 1993. pp. 2–3.

conflicting territorial claims from Bosnia to Mindanao. Most important, the efforts of the West to promote its values of democracy and liberalism as universal values, to maintain its military predominance and to advance its economic interests engender countering responses from other civilizations. Decreasingly able to mobilize support and form coalitions on the basis of ideology, governments and groups will increasingly attempt to mobilize support by appealing to common religion and civilization identity.

The clash of civilizations thus occurs at two levels. At the micro-level, adjacent groups along the fault lines between civilizations struggle, often violently, over the control of territory and each other. At the macro-level, states from different civilizations compete for relative military and economic power, struggle over the control of international institutions and third parties, and competitively promote their particular political and religious values.

The Torn Countries

In the future, as people differentiate themselves by civilization, countries with large numbers of peoples of different civilizations, such as the Soviet Union and Yugoslavia, are candidates for dismemberment. Some other countries have a fair degree of cultural homogeneity but are divided over whether their society belongs to one civilization or another. These are torn countries. Their leaders typically wish to pursue a bandwagoning strategy and to make their countries members of the West, but the history, culture and traditions of their countries are non-Western. The most obvious and prototypical torn country is Turkey. The late twentieth-century leaders of Turkey have followed in the Attatürk tradition and defined Turkey as a modern, secular, Western nation state. They allied Turkey with the West in NATO and in the Gulf War; they applied for membership in the European Community. At the same time, however, elements in Turkish society have supported an Islamic revival and have argued that Turkey is basically a Middle Eastern Muslim society. In addition, while the elite of Turkey has defined Turkey as a Western society, the elite of the West refuses to accept Turkey as such. Turkey will not become a member of the European Community, and the real reason, as President Özal said, "is that we are Muslim and they are Christian and they don't say that." Having rejected Mecca, and then being rejected by Brussels, where does Turkey look? Tashkent may be the answer. The end of the Soviet Union gives Turkey the opportunity to become the leader of a revived Turkic civilization involving seven countries from the borders of Greece to those of China. Encouraged by the West, Turkey is making strenuous efforts to carve out this new identity for itself.

During the past decade Mexico has assumed a position somewhat similar to that of Turkey. Just as Turkey abandoned its historic opposition to Europe and attempted to join Europe, Mexico has stopped defining itself by its opposition to the United States and is instead attempting to imitate the United States and to join it in the North American Free Trade Area. Mexican leaders are engaged in the great task of redefining Mexican identity and have introduced fundamental economic reforms that eventually will lead to fundamental political change. In 1991 a top adviser to President Carlos Salinas de Gortari described at length to me all the changes the Salinas government was making. When he finished, I remarked: "That's most impressive. It seems to me that basically you want to change Mexico from a Latin American country into a North American country." He looked at me with surprise and exclaimed: "Exactly! That's precisely what we are trying to do, but of course we could never say so publicly." As his remark indicates, in Mexico as in Turkey, significant elements in society resist the redefinition of their country's identity. In Turkey, European-oriented leaders have to make gestures to Islam (Özal's pilgrimage to Mecca); so also Mexico's North American-oriented leaders have to make gestures to those who hold Mexico to be a Latin American country (Salinas' Ibero-American Guadalajara summit).

Historically Turkey has been the most profoundly torn country. For the United States, Mexico is the most immediate torn country. Globally the most important torn country is Russia. The question of whether Russia is part of the West or the leader of a distinct Slavic-Orthodox civilization has been a recurring one in Russian history. That issue was obscured by the communist victory in Russia, which imported a Western ideology, adapted it to Russian conditions and then challenged the West in the name of that ideology. The dominance of communism shut off the historic debate over Westernization versus Russification. With communism discredited Russians once again face that question.

President Yeltsin is adopting Western principles and goals and seeking to make Russia a "normal" country and a part of the West. Yet both the Russian elite and the Russian public are divided on this issue. Among the more moderate dissenters, Sergei Stankevich argues that Russia should reject the "Atlanticist" course, which would lead it "to become European, to become a part of the world economy in rapid and organized fashion, to become the eighth member of the Seven, and to put particular emphasis on Germany and the United States as the two dominant members of the Atlantic alliance." While also rejecting an exclusively Eurasian policy, Stankevich nonetheless argues that Russia should give priority to the protection of Russians in other countries, emphasize its Turkic and Muslim connections, and promote "an appreciable redistribution of our resources, our options, our ties, and our interests in favor of Asia, of the eastern direction." People of this persuasion criticize Yeltsin for subordinating Russia's interests to those of the West, for reducing Russian military strength, for failing to support traditional friends such as Serbia, and for pushing economic and political reform in ways injurious to the Russian people. Indicative of this trend is the new popularity of the ideas of Petr Savitsky, who in the 1920s argued that Russia was a unique Eurasian civilization.[3] More extreme dissidents voice much more blatantly nationalist, anti-Western and anti-Semitic views, and urge Russia to redevelop its military strength and to establish closer ties with China and Muslim countries. The people of Russia are as divided as the elite. An opinion survey in European Russia in the spring of 1992 revealed that 40 percent of the public had positive attitudes toward the West and 36 percent had negative attitudes. As it has been for much of its history, Russia in the early 1990s is truly a torn country.

To redefine its civilization identity, a torn country must meet three requirements. First, its political and economic elite has to be generally supportive of and enthusiastic about this move. Second, its public has to be willing to acquiesce in the redefinition. Third, the dominant groups in the recipient civilization have to be willing to embrace the convert. All three requirements in large part exist with respect to Mexico. The first two in large part exist with respect to Turkey. It is not clear that any of them exist with respect to Russia's joining the West. The conflict between liberal democracy and Marxism-Leninism was between ideologies which, despite their major differences, ostensibly shared ultimate goals of freedom,

---

3   Sergei Stankevich, "Russia in Search of Itself," *The National Interest*, Summer 1992, pp. 47–51; Daniel Schneider, "A Russian Movement Rejects Western Tilt," *Christian Science Monitor*, Feb. 5, 1993, pp. 5–7.

equality and prosperity. A traditional, authoritarian, nationalist Russia could have quite different goals. A Western democrat could carry on an intellectual debate with a Soviet Marxist. It would be virtually impossible for him to do that with a Russian traditionalist. If, as the Russians stop behaving like Marxists, they reject liberal democracy and begin behaving like Russians but not like Westerners, the relations between Russia and the West could again become distant and conflictual.[4]

· ·

Quest for Legal Sovereignty

The law is often best understood through experience. In *Law and Identity*, Linda Medcalf examines the relationship between lawyers and American Indians in Washington State. Although the relationship with American Indians has been complicated, there has been a stability in behavioral expectations that center on what the law is and how we can act within the legal framework. In this reading, the lawyers pursue a strategy for legal sovereignty for American Indians: the ability to look and act like a government with other state and federal government agencies. The assumption the lawyers make is that power can be earned by giving up nonlegal cultural practices and behaviors. If the law is like a river flowing around us, then this assumption of assimilation is akin to jumping in headfirst. A fundamental question must be examined in this study: As one goes through the steps toward legal sovereignty, does this process alter the state of mind or constitution of the individual and the group?

---

4   Owen Harries has pointed out that Australia is trying (unwisely in his view) to become a torn country in reverse. Although it has been a full member not only of the West but also of the ABCA military and intelligence core of the West, its current leaders are in effect proposing that it defect from the West, redefine itself as an Asian country and cultivate close ties with its neighbors. Australia's future, they argue, is with the dynamic economies of East Asia. But, as I have suggested, close economic cooperation normally requires a common cultural base. In addition, none of the three conditions necessary for a torn country to join another civilization is likely to exist in Australia's case.

···

from

The Quest for Sovereignty[5]

Law and Identity: Lawyers, Native Americans
and Legal Practice. Sage, 1978. 46–62.

Linda Medcalf

Given the lawyer's definitions of Native Americans' problems and possibilities, the first step on the road to solutions seems obvious. In order to break the powerlessness cycle, regaining control of one's own affairs—i.e., self-sufficiency—is necessary. Here the concept of "tribal sovereignty" appears to the lawyers to be made to order. Though the concept is "fundamentally of Western origin," the tribes had been dealt with in such terms by Anglo society for many years. Moreover, it is a term with which lawyers are familiar and able to work. Though hundreds of pages of legal and social scientific work had been devoted to discussing, analyzing, and trying to define "sovereign," the concern here is with what it had come to mean in Native American affairs. More specifically, the activity of lawyers representing Native Americans in pursuit of tribal sovereignty will illuminate what it is by how it is practiced.

Quasi-Sovereignty

A Short History
In Native American legal history, the tribal sovereignty concept is actually "quasi-sovereign," because the federal government has the power to alter Native American status should it so desire. Essentially, the term covers the very complicated legal status of tribal governments vis-a-vis other governmental units and citizens. With respect to the federal government and its agents, Native American units retain every right of self-government that has not been taken away or altered by congressional action. As one lawyer explained it, "There is no law saying Indians could or could not do that. The rights not taken away remain with the tribe." With regard to state governments and their agents, such as cities and counties, Native American units are sovereign unless Congress has given the states the jurisdiction or power

---

5   Linda Medcalf, "The Quest for Sovereignty," *Law and Identity: Lawyers, Native Americans and Legal Practice*, pp. 46-62. Copyright © 1978 by SAGE Publications. Reprinted with permission.

to interfere. In practice, however, states often take a more aggressive role. For example:

> Today states may assert authority over Indian tribes in the absence of Congressional prohibition, provided that there is no interference with a recognized right of tribal self-government or the exercise of federal authority.

Thus tribal sovereignty has come to be the residue of self-government rights left to the tribes by Congress plus those rights which have been successfully asserted by the tribes and recognized as such by specific states.

Much of the long history of the United States' relationship with Native American tribes consists of altering tribes' legal status to accord with changing policy goals. Since the judicial branch of the federal government recognized tribes as only quasi-sovereign, Congress and the executive could tamper with the degree and nature of powers and rights left with the tribes. As is well known, federal policy has swung back and forth from assimilation and termination to separation and recondition of cultural values. Present federal policy is, at least rhetorically, supportive of Native American sovereignty (often defined as the right of self-determination, a well known phrase with which, theoretically, the United States deals with other governments as well). An example is the Jackson resolution:

> The Jackson resolution would establish that it will be the policy of the federal government to "give Indians the freedom and encouragement to develop their individual family, and community potential and to determine their own future to the maximum extent possible." It further states that "maximizing opportunities for Indian control and self-determination shall be a major goal of our national Indian policy."

This resolution is Congressional recognition of the shift in national policy expressed by President Richard Nixon in 1968. If followed by action consistent with its rhetoric, it could greatly aid the movement for Native American self-determination.

From the perspective of lawyers who represent Native Americans, tribal sovereignty is more vital than our shifting national policy on the issue suggests. As one lawyer stated, "Self determination is the road to salvation. It means to be able to control their own destiny." Tribal sovereignty, with or without supporting national policy, informs activity: "Even if the doctrine … were a legal fiction, judicial enunciation of the doctrine has given Indians a theory today upon which to build more viable systems of self-government and economic development." If Native Americans are to solve their problems, according to their lawyers, they must first be able to control their own destiny and operate like a government. For example:

> Not withstanding the fact that there are many questions concerning the scope of Indian sovereignty, one general conclusion emerges: It is necessary for Indian tribal governments to examine past actions which have limited their sovereignty so that they may anticipate and prepare for similar actions in the future. Unless tribal governments exercise or otherwise clearly identify those powers which they still possess, they run the risk of losing what remains of tribal sovereignty—which essentially is the right of self-government.
>
> If Indians an non-Indians truly aspire to the goal of "Indian self-determination," tribal sovereignty must be recognized. From the legal viewpoint, the concept and practice of Native American tribal sovereignty must be maintained.

Necessary Prerequisites

In other words, "it is not only the theoretical power that is important, but the exercise of that power. Through recognition of the concept of tribal sovereignty is helpful, by itself is not enough. As one lawyer stated, "The legal rights have been there many years, but legal rights are not automatic. The law is not self asserting." In order for tribal sovereignty to do the job lawyers see it as capable of doing, it must be exercised through aggressive assertion and utilization of sovereignty rights on the part of tribes. Assertion and utilization require positive action. The law of sovereign rights is truly the activity of exercising those rights. But before tribes act, they must want to do so. They must become ready and willing to take control of their won destiny. In the lawyers' words, Native Americans' political consciousness must be raised.

Simultaneously, the tribes need willing and competent legal aid in order to assert their legal rights, both in the courts and elsewhere. As one of the attorneys interviewed put it: "Lawyers have played a major role as lobbyists and legislators … Lawyers are a critical part of our system so if you want a major piece of legislation, you want to get a good lawyer on it." In order to translate the theory of tribal sovereignty into practice, the attorneys feel two prerequisites must be met. First, there must be clients desirous of acting. And secondly, there must be attorneys willing and able to represent such clients.

Are the clients ready? According to one lawyer, "The movement for tribal sovereignty is the biggest movement right now." He explained that, at least in Washington and most of the Pacific Northwest, fishing rights cases are the impetus for this movement. The advent of the oil discoveries in 1966 played a similar roll in awakening the political consciousness of the Alaskan Indians. The catalytic factor may vary from case to case, but natural resources are almost always involved. But one lawyer argued that the change in attitude by Native Americans

> was part of a world wide system of minority assertiveness. The increasing egalitarian notions of the 50s and 60s has also hit Indian communities. it is not exactly the same and doesn't show up the same way, but it is part of the world wide egalitarian movement. Regardless of cause, the attorneys perceive an increase in Native American political consciousness.

However, because of self-determination is essentially legal, tribes need professional advice on how to proceed. In the past, competent legal representation has been unavailable to the Indians "for all the old reasons, such as lack of funds, racism, lack of legal knowledge, etc." But now things are changing:

> Legal representation of Indians was very bad until about five to seven or eight years ago. Now it is markedly improved. This is true generally for all minorities but with Indians it came later. Indians are usually represented quite well to excellently now. That has combined with the assertiveness of Indians insisting on their rights and on following legal and other measures to assert those rights—it could be that assertiveness is partly a result of the lawyers—a kind of reciprocal thing.

This combination of raised political consciousness and increasing availability of competent and willing legal counsel makes the present quest for tribal sovereignty viable.

The Components of Tribal Sovereignty

But what does sovereignty of self-determination actually mean to these lawyers? What does the activity of the pursuit of tribal sovereignty reveal? The attorneys' definition of sovereignty will become clearer by looking at the components they believe to be central and are therefore engaged in asserting and utilizing. There are presently three main areas in which lawyers are busily aiding tribes in the assertion of governmental powers: (1) jurisdictional questions involving control over Native Americans and any others who enter reservation boundaries; (2) licensing, taxing and zoning powers to maintain control over their land; and (3) the assertion of treaty rights generally relation to resources such as fish, game, water, minerals, etc. By examining each in turn, what the quest for sovereignty means in terms of activity will begin to emerge.

Jurisdiction

One of the major areas of legal concern is the expansion of sovereignty by the assertion of jurisdiction. The standard definition of "jurisdiction" is:

> 1. *Law*. The legal power, right, or authority to hear and determine a cause or causes. 2. Authority of a sovereign power to govern or legislate; control. 3. Sphere of authority.

But jurisdiction has taken on a very complicated pattern on reservations over the course of the years. In the criminal jurisdiction area, authority was shared for a time by the federal and tribal governments. Under the Major Crimes Act (23 Stat. 362, 385), the federal government assumed total responsibility for prosecution and punishment of several serious felonies, such as rape, murder, and kidnapping. However, this still left a large range of jurisdiction to the tribes. In 1953, in response to what Congress and some tribes saw as an inability to handle the "crime" problem (and as part of a move to terminate separate Native American entities), Native American land and over Native Americans, if the state desired to assume it. Several did, creating what is not viewed by the lawyers as a blatant invasion of tribal sovereignty. Therefore, a specific goal of many lawyers is to pass legislation to get retrocession of the Public Law 280.

During the hearings regarding the Native Bill of Rights, a portion of which related to the alteration of Public Law 280, testimony was almost unanimous in decrying the Act and supporting its repeal:

Indian groups have urged repeal of Public Law 280 because it authorizes the unilateral application of State law to all tribes without their consent and regardless of their special needs and circumstances. Many tribes have also asserted that tribal laws were unnecessarily preempted by Public Law 280 and that, as a result, they could not govern their tribal communities effectively.

The main argument against Public Law 280 was summarized by Senator Sam Ervin (Dem., N.C.), chairman of the committee, as "that the control by the State, the State having jurisdiction over the tribal lands, over the reservation, would have a tendency to prevent the desirable objective of having the tribe develop its capacity for self-government.

Following the hearings, S. 966 was enacted, creating procedures for resumption of jurisdiction. However, according to the attorneys, this still leaves too much power with the states. In order for a tribe to regain jurisdiction, the state legislature must cooperate. In Washington, lawyers representing Native Americans have not yet been able to win such cooperation. Therefore, since jurisdiction is so vitally important, legal activity continues to be directed toward returning that power to tribal governments, if not through repeal by state legislatures or the victory of a court case, then by overriding federal legislation. The bill most recently presented to the Congress supports the concept of Indian self-government because it requires action solely by the tribe—no permission from the state is needed.

One of the reasons the attorneys perceive jurisdictional resumption as so important is a concern with law and order. It is assumed that if the tribe is to be able to maintain internal order (as it must), then the lawmaking and enforcing authority must be within the tribal unit. Regaining jurisdiction includes the creation of a good criminal justice system. One lawyer explained a portion of the tasks he performs for his Native American clients as follows:

The law and order code business: There is a stock code. The definition of crimes is not too difficult. To define punishments is not too difficult. Then we have to create judges and give them responsibilities. Essentially we are making a fundamental legal system. I am presently drafting a law and order code for them.

Similarly, as part of the legal education process, law students aid in the drafting of law and order codes for the various tribes in the Seattle area. Much effort goes into drafting the codes so that each tribe will be able to assert its law and order jurisdiction. Resumption of such powers is a fundamental step in preserving tribal authority and maintaining order. But Public Law 280 "authorized the various States to assume civil and criminal jurisdiction in the Indian country." Though criminal enforcement plays an important role, civil jurisdiction is perceived to be just as vital. Areas such as adoption, domestic relations, and building and sanitation regulations are also important areas of concern. One tribal attorney stated that the tribal government would "enforce its laws against Indians and non-Indians alike in the reservation." Thus all problems and all persons should become subject to tribal jurisdiction.

Some tribes have adopted what is commonly called and "implied consent" ordinance. This is posted on reservation boundaries and states that all those who enter, by the act of entering, have agreed to abide by all tribal laws and accept tribal jurisdiction. One of the major recommendations of a study of tribal authority sponsored by the Law Enforcement Administration Association (LEAA) was that each tribe adopt such an implied consent law. The study included a draft model ordinance for tribes to utilize. Such actions are designed to lead to complete resumption of jurisdiction—civil and criminal—over all persons, "Indian and non-Indian alike," by the tribal government. Jurisdiction—control over all within certain boundaries—is a very important component of sovereignty.

Taxing and Zoning

To the attorneys, the power to tax and zone is a synonymous with "acting like the government." Though which entity has the authority to tax and zone is a jurisdictional question, it merits special treatment because lawyers representing Native Americans direct much of their activity toward the assertion of these powers. Lawyers' very definition of sovereign includes the taxation and zoning powers. Several subproblems are involved due, for example to the fact that taxing can be a method of raising revenue or of regulation, or both. For outside governmental agencies to attempt to tax Native Americans is viewed as an invasion of tribal sovereignty. Similarly, zoning holds implications regarding control of land, and thus development. Though taxing and zoning are lumped together in the lawyers' minds, they involve different activities and so will be considered separately.

In Washington State, the controversy over taxing has taken a rather peculiar form. Much space is devoted in the news to the sale of cigarettes and liquor by Native Americans. Though it may seem strange to defend such shops with arms, to the Native Americans and their lawyers the issue is one of principle. It revolves around the question of the authority of the state and federal governments to tax Native Americans and their governments. Cigarette sales involve state power. Native American sellers do not pay the state taxes on cigarettes so they can sell them fairly cheaply. The state, continuing to lose revenues, continues to attempt to collect the tax. For example, in a recent legislative session, a bill was presented proposing that a duty on cigarettes be collected upon leaving reservation boundaries. During testimony, one major Native American Lawyer, Robert Pirtle, "representing several Indian tribes, opposed the measure on grounds federal law clearly exempts the state from collecting the tax on cigarettes sold on the Indian land." If the state could tax, it could regulate or even destroy the Native American businessman.

Though the Washington cases usually involve cigarettes, the principle would apply to any business. For example:

> An enrolled member of the Hoopa Tribe has brought suit in Humboldt Superior Court seeking a declaration that businesses on the reservation are not subject to county and state taxes … The suit contends that the county is without authority to tax or regulate the Indian's business, as businesses on the reservation are regulated by the federal government and the state lacks taxing jurisdiction on the reservation.

Obviously, the lawyers' activity is to insure that one sovereign entity (in this case the state government) cannot invade the land of another sovereign entity (the tribal government) to tax or regulate its citizens. That is a power reserved to the sovereign entity over those boundaries. In another area, the state excise tax on vehicles, a stronger principle is being asserted. As the lawyer inter-viewed explained it:

> The tribe has owned vehicles for several years and each year they get a huge excise tax bill from the state. They have known for years they shouldn't have to pay that tax—why should they pay that to the state? We are a government, we shouldn't pay this … The problem came up again this year.

It was given to the tribal attorney [a new situation] and they called the Attorney General and the DMV [Department of Motor Vehicles] and made their case that we should have state exempt licenses just like any other government.

The state, of course, did not agree. However, on their attorney's advice and assistance, in order to assert tribal sovereignty and challenge the state's taxing power, the tribe drafted and adopted its own licensing ordinance, issued tribal license plates, and refused to pay the state tax bill. Though this case is presently in the lower courts, it is expected that similar activity will not cease.

The other side of the coin is tribal power to collect taxes for the tribe's benefit. Exemption from state taxation is one vital assertion. But sovereignty also includes the positive power to do, the exercise of power. It seems to be an axiom that governments need revenue and tribal governments are no exception: "Indians have been on a grant economy, and that is worrisome, but now taking control of things." For example, regarding cigarette taxation by the tribes, "tribal taxes collected on the sales are helping Indians take care of their high unemployment and social problems without going to the state for help." The important fact is tribal assertion of the exclusive power to tax and collect such revenues for tribal benefit. Similarly, it can be expected that other forms of taxation, such as the licensing ordinance, will also be asserted beyond sovereign community to the positive power to tax and, in this case, issue tribal licenses and permits.

Equally important to the attorneys is the power of zoning, which includes the ability to regulate land usage and development possibilities. For example, in discussing the Alaskan case, one attorney noted: "It [the borough] also has zoning power which is very important because now oil is going to have to go to the municipal corporation and get permission to locate an oil well someplace, or permission to build a road, etc." Because zoning gives the governing authority control over land use and development, the possibility of destruction by outsiders merely interested in quick profit is fore-stalled. As one attorney stated: "It [the tribe] must maintain control over the land usage on the reservation."

A report on a recent zoning case deserves quoting at length, since it covers many of the is-sues lawyers feel are important:

A decision on whether the City of Palm Springs has the right to control economic development on the Agua Caliente

Reservation through city zoning laws is under consideration by the Ninth Circuit Court, following a hearing here in mid-January … The court battles started as soon as the city began enforcing its zoning laws on Indian land. Among other arguments, the city claims that PL280 gives the right to do this.

As things now stand, both the city and the Agua Calientes have legally constituted planning commissions and separate zoning ordinances. At first it was thought the two commissions could work cooperatively but the city has consistently denied the right of the Indian commission to final approval on matters affecting Indian land …

The primary issues the court is being asked to decide are: the legality of including trust land in the city, whether the city zoning ordinances constitute unlawful interference with tribal government, and whether application of the zoning ordinances is inconsistent with federal law … Simpson [tribal attorney] also maintains in his brief that the Agua Client Tribal Council not only has a right but a duty to control development of their land for the tribe's best interests and they are entitled to do so without state interference. He presents a strong argument that this right was not affected by PL 280. Finally, he argues that the zoning attempts are "inconsistent with performance by the United States trustee under the supremacy clause of the Federal Constitution."

With the help of expert planning consultants, lawyers engage in the very important activity of drafting zoning ordinances, building and sanitation codes, and procedures for granting zoning variances and building permits. Without such power, Native American governments will lose control of reservation lands to outside encroachments (and, usually, destruction).

In sum, to the lawyers, the very essence of sovereignty lies in the power to tax and zone. Assertion and utilization of taxing and zoning powers includes both the exemption from outside interference and the positive exercise of such powers by the tribal units. To the attorneys, a government must have exclusive control over the land within its boundaries, regardless of ownership, if it is to actually be a government. That control is perceived to be best exercised through taxation and zoning powers.

Treaty Rights and Economic Resources

Consistent with and underlying these components of sovereignty is the perceived need to regain control and pursue development of the economic resources of the tribes. According o the attorneys, it is extremely difficult to assert and maintain sovereignty without an economic base. There is a need both for tribal resources and for employment. Political and economic development must be simultaneous. When the "economic situation [is] settled, some other things could take place." In order to settle the economic situation, assertion of sovereignty based on treaty rights is required. Questions of jurisdiction and of taxing and zoning are vital to the attempt to increase economic resources. But the assertion of treaty rights goes beyond to the acquisition and control of the natural economic resources (such as water, minerals, timber, game and fish, etc.) available to Native American governments.

In Washington, the most visible and long running controversy centers on the extend of fishing rights. Most lawyers who represent Native Americans there work on a fishing rights case at one time or another. The most recent case, U.S. v. Washington, commonly called the "Boldt decision," is a great victory for the Native Americans and their lawyers. The ruling expands the previously established Native American exemption from state regulation within reservation boundaries to all usual and accustomed fishing areas of the "treaty tribes," and guarantees Native Americans 50% of the catch (following the taking of all fish necessary for ceremonial purposes). As the chairman of the Indian Fisheries Commission state: "Judge Boldt's decision has given us an economic base where the state has not been able to do that." In other words, all activity expended in pursuit of treaty rights has been worth it. The Boldt decision has strengthened tribal sovereignty. While it was in the making, Native American political consciousness was raised and tribes were solidified. But most importantly, the prerequisite for maintaining and developing as a tribe—an economic base—is now possible.

Just as important, from the lawyers' viewpoint, is the portion of the Boldt decision which rules that the state cannot regulate any Indian fishing, on or off the reservation. The state cannot interfere with treaty rights; in other words, it must recognize Native American sovereignty in this respect: "The Judge held that the tribe, 'as a government,' can regulate their fishermen off reservation without any regulation by the state. The real work is implementing the decision." As with taxing and zoning, the point is both to rid the tribe of outside interference and to exercise power positively. But it is also vital to have economic independence and resources. In the fishing rights cases, all these components were combined and won. The right to fish without state regulation and the concomitant power to make and enforce their own fishing regulations for their own members both on and off reservation is a vital recognition of tribal sovereignty. It may also provide income, an economic base which can be utilized to consolidate and further these gains.

It is not only fishing rights that are now being successfully asserted. Much legal activity is presently aimed at claiming or controlling any and all economic resources to which treaty tribes are entitled. Not all tribes have access to fish. The major point in all these cases is to remove state interference and regulation. Treaty rights are so valuable that activity is directed at maintaining them even if the underlying land has been sold or otherwise lost. For example, a recent judicial decision stated that even though the Klamaths had sold their land, their right to hunt and fish in their original domain was not sacrificed. The same point was expressed in a recent Puyallup case. The court ruled that even though most of the Puyallup reservation has been sold (an is now within the city limits of Tacoma), Native Americans retain in the treaty rights to that land. This includes hunting, fishing or selling untaxed cigarettes in Tacoma. Presumably, following the Boldt decision, tribal governments would make and enforce regulations covering these treaty rights and the Native Americans engaged in exercising them.

The states, however, are not the only entities interfering with tribes' control over economic resources. Prior to the move for self-determination, the Bureau of Indian Affairs (BIA), under the Secretary of the Interior, negotiated leases with outside parties for exploitation of Native American resources and, in general, managed such resources for the "benefit" of the tribe. Sovereignty, however, requires full control. According to one lawyer, "We are taking over Bureau monies also. The tribe is taking over the local office functions." Another lawyer described one of his functions in terms of a recent issue as follows:

> We also should make sure their [Native Americans'] land is being put to the highest and best use, besides getting the money, i.e., the coal company thing at Wind River. The requirements is that the coal company must get signatures on the leases of all the interested owners, but the land is fractionated so it won't get all the signatures so the BIA would go ahead and approve it. The people find out about it later.

> But here the Secretary said you have to deal with the Indians.
> Here the Secretary take action.

It can be safely assumed that the Secretary of the Interior did not take that action out of the goodness of his heart, but was forced to do so by the Native Americans' lawyers. In line with these lawyers' emphasis on regaining complete control over resources, lease renegotiation by the tribe and its attorneys is an important activity. Here, too, the idea is not only the necessity of possessing the resource base, but tribal control of that base as well.

Economic development is not relegated solely to traditional activities, like fishing and hunting, or to lease negotiation for better landlord terms. Lawyers are also involved in the development of new industry. For example, one lawyer put together a shake mill and was contracting with logging companies to do timber salvage. Another pointed out that all tribal owned land makes it easier to think about economic development. Since economic development is a vital part of the assertion and maintenance of sovereignty, the lawyer can assist most by performing the "function, close to the lawyer's heart, of expanding the resources available for development and the closely-related function of unraveling the legal complexities that make use of the resources almost impossible." Much of the lawyer's activity, then, centers on economic expansion.

Another vital component, therefore, in the assertion of tribal sovereignty is regaining and maintaining control of economic resources. Economic development is congruent with the activities conducted to gain jurisdiction and taxing and zoning powers: like them, control over and development of economic resources emphasize the necessity for tribal entities to rid themselves of outside interference and control. All such activities in pursuit of sovereignty are perceived by the attorneys as meshing and cumulating so as to make self-determination a reality.

Sovereignty as Power

The meaning of sovereignty as seen through legal practice revolves around the concept of power. To talk about sovereignty in this context is to explore the meaning of power as practiced by the attorneys. Lawyers' activities in pursuit of sovereignty reveal power as the ability to control and to act in vital areas. Sovereignty means control over people through jurisdictional authority and over the land through taxing and zoning. It also means control over economic rescues through the pursuit of treaty rights. Power therefore includes control over people, land, and resources both internally and as against others. It embodies an adversary notion which posits foes and balkiness and thus a need for enforcement mechanisms. The notion of power embodied in this practice centers around the ability to control; sovereign rights set one entity's ability to control against another's right to do so.

If sovereignty means control over people, land, and resources then it covers both political self-determination and economic self-sufficiency. Sometimes economic self-sufficiency is presented as a prerequisite to sovereignty, however: "In order for any minority group to enjoy the full import of its 'rights' in our success-oriented society, it must first obtain economic self-sufficiency." Much of the pursuit of treaty rights is for this very purpose—economic development. Similarly, the point on disputes over taxing and zoning can often be traced to the desire to acquire the ability to develop economically. On the other hand, it is very difficult to make these assertions without a strong governmental base. As one attorney wrote:

> It seems to me that the only way the Tribes are going to be successful in dealing with economic activity affecting the reservation, the fishing and hunting issue, or any other issue, is to take on the form of the white man's government and laws and exercise the considerable powers inherent in their own legal-governmental structures in as aggressive a way as is possible. They must push the limits of their tribal powers to govern reservation and off-reservation activities affecting them in the areas in which the reservations exist. They must be on the attack. Otherwise, the state, county, city, local flood control districts—what have you—will take on those powers and functions. The tribes will always be on the defensive— crying over spilled milk as it were—until little by little no rights of self government will exist.

In order to be "on the attack," tribes must believe themselves to be a government and act like one. In the legal mind, sovereignty, or acting like a government, centers around questions of jurisdiction and the ability to tax and zone. Sovereignty therefore requires both political self-determination and economic self-sufficiency.

The question of which comes first is irrelevant: the two go hand in hand. Political self-determination and economic self-sufficiency are essentially the same as well as independent. Their congruence extends to a point where it is difficult for lawyers to distinguish between a business and a government. The major difference is the additional power of taxing and zoning possessed by the governing unit, making the government a more powerful business unit.

Survival through Sovereignty

Underlying the quest for sovereignty, in all its guises, is the belief that such a quest is the "road to salvation." In this case, salvation means survival of Native Americans as a people. From their lawyers' point of view, such survival is impossible without progress through economic development. One attorney stated, "you have got to develop the land." Another asserted that if Native Americans "don't go outside, learn the white tools, assert yourself, and use the land," they "will not survive." Development of the land and other resources is not possible without control of them. Therefore, sovereignty must be regained. The development of sovereignty as the power to control is necessary in order to progress, which is in turn necessary in order to survive.

Without survival, the overarching goal of a "meaningful choice" would of course be irrelevant. Therefore, the first order of business is survival, which can be accomplished by replacing powerlessness with power, which can in turn be accomplished through the resumption of tribal sovereign rights. The lawyer's part in this is summed up as follows:

> an attempt is made to define certain aspects of the economic development role that reservation lawyers must confront. First, as has been indicated, there is the basic problem, rooted in deeply-held attitudes, of assisting in the definition of economic developmental goals; second, there is the function, close to the lawyer's heart, of expanding the resources available for development and the closely-related function of unraveling the legal complexities that make the use of the resources al-most impossible. Third, there is the necessity of encouraging the growth of adequate managerial expertise. The first and second activities form the basis for perceiving the necessity of asserting sovereignty and attempting to gather into the tribal unit as much power as possible. The third role is developing managerial expertise.

Letter from a Birmingham Jail

Much legislative and judicial change occurred throughout the many years of the civil rights movement. We see this change as a collective process of over one hundred years of civic identity and agency for those who were denied citizenship in the *Dred Scott* case as a legacy of slavery. As we see today,  issues of civic conflict still emanate from the unequal access to participation. From voting to running for office, or from education to opportunity in the workplace, there are many stinging examples of unfair treatment. Dr. Martin Luther King Jr. provides a clear rationale for civic change in this short excerpt.

....

from

Letter from a Birmingham Jail.

1964.[6]

Martin Luther King, Jr.

I just referred to the creation of tension as a part of the work of the nonviolent resister. This may sound rather shocking. But I must confess that I am not afraid of the word tension. I have earnestly worked and preached against violent tension, but there is a type of constructive nonviolent tension that is necessary for growth. Just as Socrates felt that it was necessary to create a tension in the mind so that individuals could rise from the bondage of myths and half-truths to the unfettered realm of creative analysis and objective appraisal,

---

6   Dr. Martin Luther King Jr., "Excerpt from: Letter from Birmingham Jail," Copyright in the public domain.

we must see the need of having nonviolent gadflies to create the kind of tension in society that will help men rise from the dark depths of prejudice and racism to the majestic heights of understanding and brotherhood. So the purpose of the direct action is to create a situation so crisis packed that it will inevitably open the door to negotiation. We, therefore, concur with you in your call for negotiation. Too long has our beloved Southland been bogged down in the tragic attempt to live in monologue rather than dialogue.

One of the basic points in your statement is that our acts are untimely. Some have asked, "Why didn't you give the new administration time to act?" The only answer that I can give to this inquiry is that the new administration must be prodded about as much as the outgoing one before it acts. We will be sadly mistaken if we feel that the election of Mr. Boutwell will bring the millennium to Birmingham. While Mr. Boutwell is much more articulate and gentle than Mr. Connor, they are both segregationists dedicated to the task of maintaining the status quo. The hope I see in Mr. Boutwell is that he will be reasonable enough to see the futility of massive resistance to desegregation. But he will not see this without pressure from the devotees of civil rights. My friends, I must say to you that we have not made a single gain in civil rights without determined legal and nonviolent pressure. History is the long and tragic story of the fact that privileged groups seldom give up their privileges voluntarily. Individuals may see the moral light and voluntarily give up their unjust posture; but as Reinhold Niebuhr has reminded us, groups are more immoral than individuals.

We know through painful experience that freedom is never voluntarily given by the oppressor; it must be demanded by the oppressed. Frankly I have never yet engaged in a direct action movement that was "well timed," according to the timetable of those who have not suffered unduly from the disease of segregation. For years now I have heard the word "Wait!" It rings in the ear of every Negro with a piercing familiarity. This "wait" has almost always meant "never." It has been a tranquilizing thalidomide, relieving the emotional stress for a moment, only to give birth to an ill-formed infant of frustration. We must come to see with the distinguished jurist of yesterday that "justice too long delayed is justice denied." We have waited for more than three hundred and forty years for our constitutional and God-given rights.

Law, Society, and Justice with D+CPAR

Critical participatory action research now includes a vast collection of powerful digital tools that can be integrated into social science and humanities research. Thus, D+CPAR is an emerging field that can provide insightful and practical academic study and can develop highly demanded skill sets in the marketplace and in public service. One such project examines the gaps in access to immigration and citizenship services in geographical communities throughout New York City. The curriculum redesign process starts by asking what you, as co-researchers, really want to do. From this inquiry, learners and the instructor can design scaffolded assignments that can build research skills through support exercises and the integration of course content. In order to get a rough sketch to be used for future mapping, our D+CPAR project began with a collection of information from neighborhoods where students lived. We then discussed what community meant to us and what minimum features of jurisdiction were important for civic equality. Through a series of cocreated online research assignments, students conducted legal research using public website tools and reflected on their findings through the examination of surveys, to show common learning, and through dialogue about what partners were needed to discuss solutions to community problems. Learners then uploaded their data onto an interactive map using a public blogging platform, and we were able to examine where gaps in access existed and identify potential partners. Two important findings have come out of this collaborative process: (1) Throughout New York, those who are most vulnerable to flooding are also the most poor; and (2) gun violence in two neighboring communities occurred most frequently around liquor stores. One student is now working on the former finding in a master's degree program, and another student is examining how social media over-reports shootings and other violent crimes, leading community members to believe there are more crimes occurring all over a neighborhood. By including learners as co-researchers for civic change, educators can conduct scholarly research and writing in the classroom with students, and learners can confront big challenges in modern communities with confidence. This is one way we hope to close the civic gap and build a larger consensus.

Politics of Land Reform

A historical tension between private property owners and the workers who provide the wealth is well documented throughout the social sciences. Through the study of social change in land reform, we want to consider when and how change occurs in this historical conflict. While we are too familiar with the violent uprising and violent counter-reaction, we wonder whether these dimensions are too rigid for intelligent civic dialogue in the twenty-first century. As you read these excerpts from Samuel Huntington's *Political Order in Changing Societies*, please consider a dialogue around how unequal groups can relate to civic change in a meaningful, inclusive, and respectful way.

....

from

The Politics of Land Reform[7]

Samuel Huntington

Patterns of land tenure obviously vary greatly from country to country and from region to region. In general, in Latin America, a relatively small number of latifundia have encompassed a large proportion of the total farm land while a large number of minifundia covered a small proportion of the total farm land. Neither large estate nor small plot has been typically farmed efficiently, and, of course, the disparity in income between the owner of one and the owner of the other has been very great. In Asia land ownership typically has not been as concentrated as in Latin America, but tenancy, absentee landlordism, and high population densities have been more prevalent. Near Eastern countries have been characterized by a high concentration of land ownership in some instances (Iraq, Iran) and by high tenancy rates in others. With the exception of tropical Africa, in one form or another the objective conditions likely to give rise to peasant unrest are common in much of the modernizing world. If, as appears likely, modernization will in due course arouse peasant aspirations to the point where these conditions are no longer tolerable, then the alternatives of revolution or land reform are very real ones for many political systems.

The saliency of land reform to politics in different countries is suggested by the data in Table 2.1. On the horizontal axis this table

---

7   Samuel Huntington, "Reform and Political Change: The Politics of Land Reform," *Political Order in Changing Societies Reform and Political Change Politics of Land Reform*, pp. 380–383, 394–396. Copyright © 1968 by Yale University Press. Reprinted with permission.

gives a rough idea of the importance of agriculture to a country's economy; on the vertical axis, it classifies countries by inequality in land distribution, the data for which are for different years for different countries and in some cases two different years for the same country. Underneath the names of most countries on the table are figures on farm tenancy and their date.

From these data it would appear that land reform is not a pressing issue in four types of countries. First, in countries which have reached a high level of economic development, agriculture has a relatively minor role, and consequently even highly inequitable patterns of land ownership do not pose substantial problems of social equality and political stability. Such is the case with virtually all the countries in the left-hand column of Table 2.1. Even in a country like Argentina, characterized by both great inequality in land ownership and a high tenancy rate, the land issue is relatively secondary since less than 30 per cent of the labor force is employed in agriculture. Italy also combines unequal ownership and high tenancy, but the problem there is, of course, largely concentrated in the southern region, and reasonably effective actions have been taken by the government to cope with it. For countries in this category land reform is only a secondary issue in politics.

Second, many countries have had or achieved long ago reasonably equitable patterns of land ownership. Many of the countries of western Europe in groups G and J fall into this category as well as into the first category of countries where agriculture is of minor importance in economic life. While accurate and comparable figures are not readily available, at least some modernizing countries not listed in the table may also fit this pattern, among them possibly Cyprus, Lebanon, Turkey, Thailand, and Indonesia.

A third category consists of those countries, mostly in tropical Africa, where traditional communal patterns of land ownership are just beginning to give way to individual proprietorship. These countries are, in a sense, one phase behind those other modernizing countries where traditional communal patterns of ownership, if they ever existed, were replaced some time ago by individual ownership and then by the concentration of ownership in relatively few hands. Depending upon the nature of the processes of individualization of land, these African countries may avoid the problems of its inequitable distribution which now plague so many other modernizing countries.

Table 2.1. Vulnerability to Agrarian Unrest

Distribution of agricultural land: Gini Index of Inequality	Percentage of labor force employed in agriculture		
	0–29%	30–59%	60% and over
.800 and over	A Australia-93(48)* Argentina-86(52) 33(52)** Italy-80(46) 24(30)	B Mexico-96(30) Chile-94(36) 13(55) Venezuela-91(56) 21(50) Costa Rica-89(50) 5(50) Ecuador-86(54) 15(54) Columbia-(86)60 12(60) Jamaica-82(43) 10(43) Uruguay-82(50) 35(51)	C Bolivia-91(50) 20(50) Iraq-88(58) Peru-88(50) Guatemala-86(50) 17(50) Brazil-84(50) 9(50) El Salvador-83(50) 15(50) Egypt-81(52) 12(39)
.700–.799	D New Zealand-77(49) 22(50) Puerto Rico-74(59) 4(59) United Kingdom-71(50) 45(50) United States-71(50) 20(59)	E Dominican Rep-79(50) 21(50) Cuba-79(45) 54(45) Spain-78(29) 44(50) Greece-75(30) 18(39) Austria-74(51) 11(51) Panama-74(61) 12(61)	F Honduras-76(32) 17(52) Nicaragua-76(50) Libya-70(60) 9(60)

50   Section Two

Distribution of agricultural land: Gini Index of Inequality	Percentage of labor force employed in agriculture		
	0–29%	30–59%	60% and over
.500–.699	G West Germany-67(49) 6(49) Norway-67(59) 8(50) Luxembourg-64(50) 19(50) Netherlands-61(50) 53(48) Belgium-59(59) 62(58) France-58(48) 26(46) Sweden-58(44) 19(44)	H Mexico-69(60) Taiwan-65(30) 40(48) Finland-60(50) 2(50) Ireland-60(60) 3(32) Philippines-59(48) 37(48) Philippines-53(60)	I S. Vietnam-67(35) 20(50) Egypt-67(64) Iran-65(60) India-63(54) 53(31) W. Pakistan-61(60) India-59(61) E. Pakistan-51(60)
.499 and below	J Switzerland-49(39) 19(44) Canada-49(31) 7(51) Denmark-46(59) 4(49)	K Japan-47(60) 3(60) Taiwan-46(60) Poland-45(60)	L Yugoslavia-44(50)

Source: Bruce, M. Russett et al., *World Handbook of Political and Social Indicators* (New Haven, Yale University Press, 1964). Tables 50, 69, 70; Hung-chao Tai, "Land Reform in Developing Countries: Tenure Defects and Political Response" (Unpublished Paper, Harvard University, Center for International Affairs, 1967).
*Gini Index and date.
**Farms on rented land as percentage of total farms and date.

A final, fourth category of countries where land reform is not a salient problem includes those where effective, thoroughgoing reforms have been carried out by revolution or otherwise in recent years. These include all the communist countries which have collectivized agriculture plus Poland and Yugoslavia, which have created highly equitable patterns of individual land ownership. Among the noncommunist countries, the post-World War II reforms in Japan and Taiwan at least temporarily removed the land question as a major political issue. In some measure the same result has been obtained through revolution in Mexico and Bolivia, although the problems of the inefficiency of the *ejido* and tendencies toward the reconcentration of ownership continue to plague the former country.

In the remainder of the modernizing world, land reform has a high saliency to politics. Land reform problems, it may be predicted, are likely to be most critical in those seven countries in group C which combine high inequalities of land ownership with substantial agricultural labor forces. In 1950 Bolivia had what was probably the highest Gini index of inequality in land ownership in the world and also substantial tenancy; in 1952 Bolivia had its agrarian revolution. In 1958 Iraq also had a highly unequal pattern of land ownership; the same year a modernizing military junta overthrew the old regime and instituted a program of land reforms. In El Salvador and Peru, with similar inequality, reform governments, with the active support of the United States, made major efforts to introduce land reforms in 1961 and 1964. The governments of Guatemala and Brazil also attempted to inaugurate major land reforms in 1954 and 1964, respectively, only to be overthrown by military insurrections. In Egypt the Nasser reforms reduced the index from .81 in 1952 to .67 in 1964. In all six countries apart from Bolivia land reform remained a major issue in the mid-1960s.

In Colombia, in the early 1960s the "social group which stood to benefit most from the law—Colombia's small tenant farmers, sharecroppers, minifundio holders and landless laborers—took only a small and indirect part in its adoption." Some land invasions did occur, but only on a relatively small scale. In Venezuela the ideological commitment and political leadership of Betancourt were the necessary complement to the mild land invasions. In Iran there was no peasant violence or extra legal activity at all. In this case, like Colombia, the leaders pushing reform were more concerned about the possible major violence in the future than actual minor violence in the past. "I do not wish to be a prophet of doom," one Colombian legislator declared: "but if the next Congress fails to produce an Agrarian Reform, revolution will be inevitable." "Divide your lands or face revolution—or death," Prime Minister Amini warned the Iranian elite.[8]

---

8   *Hirschman*, pp. 142, 157; Prime Minister Amini, quoted by Jay Walz, *New York Times*, May 30, 1961, p. 2.

"Land reform," Neale has observed, "does not make new men of peasants. New men make land reforms."[9] In the absence of revolution, the new men are initially usually from the non-peasant classes. The effectiveness of land reform, however it is initiated, nonetheless depends upon the active and eventually organized participation of the peasants. Mobilization of peasants is not necessary to start land reform, but land reform, to be successful, must stimulate the mobilization and organization of the peasants. Reform laws only become effective when they are institutionalized in organizations committed to making them effective. Two organizational links between government and peasants are necessary if land reform is to become a reality.

First, in almost all cases, the government has to create a new and adequately financed administrative organization well-staffed with expert talent committed to the cause of reform. In most countries where land reform is a crucial issue, the Ministry of Agriculture is a weak, lethargic entity, with little commitment to modernization and reform, and often quite subservient to the established agricultural interests. An indifferent bureaucracy can make reform a nullity. The failure of land reform in several districts in India, for instance, was ascribed in one survey to two causes: "one is faulty legislation itself, and the second is the negative attitude of the government officials at slate, district, block or village levels. With the exception of Aligarh, no serious attempt was made to enforce the enacted land reform legislation."[10] Virtually all effective land reforms thus involve the creation of an agrarian reform institute. Where such institutes are not created, as was generally the case in India, the reforms tend to become ineffective. In addition, it is also often necessary to mobilize a substantial bureaucratic-force to implement the reform in the countryside. The Japanese land reform required the assistance of some 400,000 people to purchase and transfer 2,000,000 hectares and to rewrite 4,000,000 leases. The reform in Taiwan required an administrative force of some 33,000 officials. In the Philippines and in Iran the army has been employed to help implement the reform.[11] In India, in contrast, in the

---

9   Walter G. Neale, *Economic Change in Rural India* (New Haven, Yale University Press, 1962), p. 258.

10   Wolf Ladejinsky, *A Study on Tenurial Conditions in Packaya Districts* (New Delhi, Government of India Press, 1965), p. 9.

11   J. Lossing Buck, "Progress of Land Reform in Asian Countries," in Walter Frochlich, ed., *Land Tenure, Industrialization and Social Stability: Experience and Prospects in Asia* (Milwaukee, Marquette University Press, 1961), p. 84.

early 1960s only about 6,000 full-time workers were concerned with land reform.

The second organizational requirement of land reform is the organization of the peasants themselves. Concentrated power can enact land reform decrees, but only expanded power can make those decrees into reality. While peasant participation may not be necessary to pass legislation, it is necessary to implement legislation. In democratic countries, in particular, land reform laws may be passed in deference to public opinion or ideological commitment. They often remain unenforced because of the absence of peasant organizations to participate in their implementation. "The clue to the failure of rural development," it was argued in India, "lies in this, that it cannot be administered, it has to be organized. While administration is something which the civil service can take care of, rural development is a political task, which the administration cannot undertake."[12] Peasant leagues, peasant associations, peasant cooperatives are necessary to insure the continued vitality of land reform. Whatever their declared functions, the fact of organization creates a new center of power in the countryside. De Tocqueville's democratic science of association brings a new political resource into rural politics, counterbalancing the social status, economic wealth, and advanced education which had been the principal sources of power of the landowning class.

The creation of peasant associations, consequently, is a political act, and it is most often and most effectively performed by political parties, who have an interest in mobilizing peasant support and firmly binding the peasants to their party through the mechanisms of peasant organizations. Virtually every strong political party in a modernizing country is closely affiliated with a peasant organization. Such organization clearly serves the interests of the party leaders, but it also serves the interests of the peasants.

> Whatever power the peasants gain [one comparative analysis has concluded], it will tend with time to exert a conservative influence on the national government, for, as small proprietors they have a high regard for private property. But most important to the growth of power among the rural masses is the phenomenon of peasant syndicate organizations which

---

12   *The Economic Weekly* (Bombay), Feb. 1964, p. 156, quoted by Wayne Wilcox, "The Pakistan Coup D'Etat of 1958," *Pacific Affairs*, 38 (Summer 1965), 153.

tend to accompany agrarian reform. The formation of these interest groups may well prove to be the most important outcome of many agrarian reform movements.[13]

Reform, in short, becomes real only when it becomes organized. Peasant organization is political action. Effective peasant organization comes with effective political parties.

....

DISCUSSION QUESTIONS

1. Are landowners motivated purely by inhuman drives for wealth and power?

2. Are peasants ill adapted for the social world where power and wealth reside?

3. Can a government structure, whether on paper like a constitution or in the daily habits and practices of residents, really cause or prevent violence between these two groups?

Meet Asmaa: In Reflection

This section has aimed to demonstrate the importance of identity to prompting civic action. Students are too often limited in what they think is possible and what changes can be made with their contributions, both big and small. In the classroom, we have worked to empower students to recognize their inherent skills and abilities and how they can be applied to different social movements and issues the students care about. When asked what skills they can bring, one student replied, "Well, I have a big mouth." How can that tool be used to spread the word about social issues and drive support for a cause you care about? This YouTube video introduces you to Asmaa Mahfouz. What tools did she have at her disposal? A video camera and a big mouth. And what was she able to do with that? Spark a revolution.

---

13   Erasmus, p. 787.

In reflection:

It is easy to feel powerless or to believe your efforts won't amount to much or that others will do this work better. This is your life, your school, your city, your country, and ultimately your world. You have every right to want to shape it and change it. What skills do you have that you could use to make a difference?

Connecting Your Inquiry Question

Documentation is one way to track your progress as a civic agent who is developing his or her own identity. One method we ascribe to is asking for volunteers to serve as note takers. These vignettes of teaching and learning help show the democratic process in action as it occurs in your classroom from the point of view of others. We also recommend using interactive technology such as screen recording software, online survey design websites and applications, and traditional office applications like spreadsheets, charts, and graphs to help provide a visual for your progress. As you connect your inquiry question to civic change on your campus, in your community, or in your classroom, consider what feedback learners might want as they continue.

SECTION THREE

Civic Advocacy through Critical Modern Problems

So far we have examined the role of civic identity and agency for social change by looking at individual interpretations of constitutional self-government and at critical theory that provides a framework to evaluate the prospect of civic change as an individual in a complex system. We now want to consider the Constitution, law, and society from the viewpoint of exclusion. Specifically, we want to better understand how those who are excluded from legal processes regain power and engage with the civic.

INQUIRY QUESTION

We encourage you to develop an inquiry question together, centered on empirical social science.

Brown v. Board Doll Studies

One of the most fascinating, and at the time controversial, aspects of the *Brown v. Board of Education* cases was the use of social science research to prove a harm had occurred in the separation of children in education based on skin color. One of the attorneys for the plaintiffs and future Supreme Court justice, Thurgood Marshall, urged the legal team to show damages so that the legal question would be focused on how segregation could be overturned. The doctrine of separate but equal had been a hollow gesture at equality following the Civil War and subsequent amendments. The fundamental rights and due process measures in the Fourteenth Amendment gave civil rights advocates a legal venue to make the case of integration in state courts using federal law. As you think about how the doll studies informed the Supreme Court of the deep psychological and emotional pain associated with unequal access to education and citizenship, consider how segregation today continues to be a persistent problem. After viewing the image and text on the National Park Service website, answer the following question together: How can social science help provide a blueprint for integration and a more perfect union for the democracy of tomorrow?

....

from

National Parks Service, "Kenneth and Mamie Clark Doll."

Brown v. Board of Education National Historic Site, Kansas, USA.

Kenneth and Mamie Clark Doll[1]

Children's toys rarely feature in decisions issued by the US Supreme Court of the United States. Yet a humble set of baby dolls – two black, two white – played a pivotal role in what many have termed the most important legal ruling of the 20th century. This year, in commemoration of the 60th anniversary of the US Supreme Court decision to legally end segregation in public schools, one of those dolls is on display here at Brown v. Board of Education National Historic Site. This is the doll's story.

---

1   National Parks Service, "Kenneth and Mamie Clark Doll," Copyright in the Public Domain.

For Thurgood Marshall, chief counsel for the National Association for the Advancement of Colored People (NAACP), the legal landscape looked daunting in 1951. School segregation was mandated by law in 17 states, practiced in the nation's capital and countless other school districts, and seemingly blessed by the 55-year-old separate but equal doctrine decreed by the US Supreme Court in Plessy v. Ferguson. In prior cases, the NAACP had sought relief by demonstrating the almost universal inequality of segregated schools. But now, the lawyers of the NAACP sought to convince the US Supreme Court that segregation in and of itself was unconstitutional. To make their case, Marshall and his team of lawyers needed something that provided overwhelming proof to demonstrate that equal educational opportunities for African Americans was impossible to achieve in a segregated system no matter how equal the facilities be.

To mount their attack on the belief that African American children were different from white children and unworthy of sitting side by side with them in a classroom, Marshall and his legal team relied upon the work of a group of social scientists who had been studying the effect of segregation on black children. In preparation for the Briggs v. Elliott case, the first of the five cases argued that would make their way to the US Supreme Court as *Brown v. Board of Education*, Marshall asked Kenneth and Mamie Clark, both of whom held doctorates in psychology, to repeat experiments with school children from Clarendon County, South Carolina they had conducted in New York City in the 1930s. In the experiment, the Clarks handed black children four dolls. The dolls were identical except that two had a dark-colored skin and two had light-colored skin. The Clarks asked the children questions such as which dolls were "nice" and which were "bad" and "which doll is most like you?"

The results of the test showed that the majority of black children preferred the white dolls to the black dolls, the children saying the black dolls were "bad" and that the white dolls looked most like them. To the Clarks, these tests provided solid proof that enforced segregation stamped African American children with a badge of inferiority that would last the rest of their lives. The argument swayed the US Supreme Court Chief Justice Earl Warren, in writing the Court's opinion, noted that the legal separation of black children gave them "a feeling of inferiority as to their status in the community that may affect their hearts and minds in a way un-likely to ever be undone."

Because of the impact on the Court's decision, the symbol and lightning rod for the Brown case has become the doll tests conducted by the Clarks. Therefore, not surprising, if asked what object would they most like to have in their museum collection, *Brown v. Board of Education* National Historic Site would answer the Clark dolls. Last year, the park received a call out of the blue asking if they would be interested in acquiring one of the dolls. A pair had been given by Dr. Clark to one of his students who later passed them on to one of her close friends to be used as toys for her children. While the white doll has been lost to time, the black doll remained. The original diaper was gone and the face now had a green tint after years of being exposed to sunlight. Park staff researched the story about the doll's journey and then conducted a close examination of the doll comparing it to photographs of those used by the Clarks. Staff breathed a collective sigh of relief when everything checked out. *Brown v. Board of Education* NHS is preparing to put the doll on exhibit this year, making this important symbol of one of the most transformative laws in American history available for all to see.

....

Power of Self-Definition

Patricia Hill Collins presents a powerful argument for the age-old problem of defining knowledge and who gets to participate in the naming process. The power to write, from an authentic point of view, is a form of resistance that can transform civic institutions and serve as a reminder to the collective of the importance of individual protections. As black women as a group continue to fight for social and political equality, what universal truths of self-definition and individual expression arise from the struggle for freedom? What steps have writers taken in the past that can help guide individuals who feel excluded, who have been denied access, or who have unequal power in formal civic institutions? We encourage you to integrate this reading into the dialogue you began around stereotypes and explore the different meanings of community and of the civic itself.

....

from

The Voices of Black Women Writers[2]

During the summer of 1944, recent law school graduate Pauli Murray returned to her California apartment and found the following anonymous note from the "South Crocker Street Property Owner's Association" tacked to her door: "We … wish to inform you the flat you now occupy … is restricted to the white or Caucasian race only. … We intend to uphold these restrictions, therefore we ask that you vacate the above mentioned flat … within seven days" (1987, 253). Murray's response was to write. She remembers: "I was learning that creative expression is an integral part of the equipment needed in the service of a compelling cause; it is another form of activism. Words poured from my typewriter" (p. 255).

Increased literacy among African-Americans has provided new opportunities for Black women to transform former institutional sites of domination such as scholarship and literature into institutional sites of resistance. Trudier Harris (1988) suggests that a community of Black women writers has emerged since 1970, one in which African-American women engage in dialogue among one another in order to explore formerly taboo subjects. Black feminist literary criticism is documenting the intellectual and personal space created for African-American women in this emerging body of ideas (Washington 1980, 1982; Tate 1983; Evans 1984; Christian 1985; McDowell 1985; Pryse and Spillers 1985; O'Neale 1986). Especially noteworthy are the ways in which this emerging community of Black women writers builds on former themes and approaches of the Black women's blues tradition (Williams 1979) and of earlier Black women writers (Cannon 1988). Also key are the new themes raised by contemporary Black women writers. For example, Trudier Harris (1988) contends that a variety of taboos are violated in contemporary Black women's literature, among them the taboos that Black women were not allowed to leave their children, have interracial affairs, have lesbian relationships, be the victims of incest, or generally escape the confining image of

---

2   Patricia Hill Collins, Selection from "The Power of Self-Definition," *Black Feminist Thought: Knowledge, Consciousness, and the Politics of Empowerment*, pp. 119–126. Copyright © by Taylor & Francis Group. Reprinted with permission.

"long-suffering commitment to Black people." In all, the emerging work of this growing community potentially offers another safe space where Black women can articulate a self-defined standpoint.

Not everyone agrees that Black women writers are using the full range of their voices to create safe spaces. In discussing the potential for systems of domination to harness the creative potential of Black music, Angela Davis observes, "some of the superstars of popular-musical culture today are unquestionably musical genuises, but they have distorted the Black music tradition by brilliantly developing its form while ignoring its content of struggle and freedom" (1989, 208). Black literary critic Sondra O'Neale suggests that a similar process may be affecting Black women's writing. "Where are the Angela Davises, Ida B. Wellses, and Daisy Bateses of black feminist literature?" she asks (1986,144). O'Neale contends that one of the tasks of the Black woman critic is to assess whether contemporary Black women's literature reveals those strengths that have furthered Black women's survival. "Lamentably," O'Neale points out, "we are still seeing the black women in roles that the prevailing cultural manipulators ascribe to her—always on the fringes of society, always alone" (p. 153).

The specialized thought of contemporary Black feminist writers and scholars should be able to draw on the long-standing Afrocentric tradition of struggle in order to produce "progressive art." As Angela Davis observes, "progressive art can assist people to learn not only about the objective forces at work in the society in which they live, but also about the intensely social character of their interior lives. Ultimately it can propel people toward social emancipation" (1989, 200). This type of art is emancipatory because it fuses thought, feeling, and action and helps its participants see their world differently and act to change it. Traditionally, everyday thought expressed in Black women's music approximated this definition of *progressive*. It remains to be seen whether the specialized thought generated by contemporary Black feminist thinkers in very different institutional locations is capable of creating safe spaces that will carry African-American women even further.

Consciousness as a Sphere of Freedom
Taken together, Black women's relationships with one another, the Black women's blues tradition, and the emerging influence of Black women writers coalesce to offer an alternative worldview to that embedded in institutional locations of domination. These three sites

offer safe spaces that nurture the everyday and specialized thought of African-American women and where Black women intellectuals can absorb ideas and experiences for the task of rearticulating Black women's experiences and infusing them with new meaning. More important, these new meanings offer African-American women potentially powerful tools to resist the controlling images of Black womanhood. Far from being a secondary concern in bringing about social change, challenging controlling images and replacing them with a Black women's standpoint is an essential component in resisting systems of race, gender, and class oppression (Thompson-Cager 1989). What are some of the fundamental themes developed in these safe spaces?

The Importance of Self-Definition

"Black groups digging on white philosophies ought to consider the source. Know who's playing the music before you dance," cautions poet Nikki Giovanni (1971, 126). Her advice is especially germane for African-American women. Giovanni suggests: "We Black women are the single group in the West intact. And anybody can see we're pretty shaky. We are … the only group that derives its identity from itself. I think it's been rather unconscious but we measure ourselves by ourselves, and I think that's a practice we can ill afford to lose" (1971, 144). Black women's survival is at stake, and creating self-definitions reflecting an independent Afrocentric feminist consciousness is an essential part of that survival.

The issue of the journey from internalized oppression to the "free mind" of a self-defined, Afrocentric feminist consciousness is a prominent theme in the works of Black women writers. Author Alexis DeVeaux notes that there is a "great exploration of the self in women's work. It's the self in relationship with an intimate other, with the community, the nation and the world" (in Tate 1983, 54). Far from being a narcissistic or trivial concern, this placement of self at the center of analysis is critical for understanding a host of other relationships. DeVeaux continues, "you have to understand what your place as an individual is and the place of the person who is close to you. You have to understand the space between you before you can understand more complex or larger groups" (p. 54).

Black women have also stressed the importance of self-definition as part of the journey from victimization to a free mind in their blues. Sherley Anne Williams's analysis of the affirmation of self in the blues make a critical contribution in understanding the blues as a Black women's text. In discussing the blues roots of Black literature, Williams notes, "the assertion of individuality and the implied assertion—as action, not mere verbal statement—of self is an important dimension of the blues" (1979, 130).

The assertion of self usually comes at the end of a song, after the description or analysis of the troublesome situation. This affirmation of self is often the only solution to that problem or situation. Nina Simone's (1985) classic blues song "Four Women" illustrates this use of the blues to affirm self. Simone sings of three Black women whose experiences typify controlling images—Aunt Sarah, the mule, whose back is bent from a lifetime of hard work; Sweet Thing, the Black prostitute who will belong to anyone who has money to buy; and Saphronia, the mulatto whose Black mother was raped late one night. Simone explores Black women's objectification as the Other by invoking the pain these three women actually feel. But Peaches, the fourth woman, is an especially powerful figure, because Peaches is angry. "I'm awfully bitter these days," Peaches cries out, "because my parents were slaves." These words and the feelings they invoke demonstrate her growing awareness and self-definition of the situation she encountered and offer to the listener, not sadness and remorse, but an anger that leads to action. This is the type of individuality Williams means—not that of talk but self-definitions that foster action.

While the theme of the journey also appears in the work of Black men, African-American women writers and musicians explore this journey toward freedom in ways that are characteristically female (Thompson-Cager 1989). Black women's journeys, though at times embracing political and social issues, basically take personal and psychological forms and rarely reflect the freedom of movement of Black men who hop "trains," "hit the road," or in other ways physically travel in order to find that elusive sphere of freedom from racial oppression. Instead, Black women's journeys often involve "the transformation of silence into language and action" (Lorde 1984, 40). Typically tied to children and/or community, fictional Black women characters search for self-definition within close geographical boundaries. Even though physical limitations confine the Black heroine's quest to a specific area, "forming complex personal relationships adds depth to her identity quest in lieu of geographical breadth" (Tate 1983, xxi). In their search for self-definition and the power of a free mind, Black heroines may remain "motionless on the outside … but inside?"

Given the physical limitations on Black women's mobility, the conceptualization of self that is part of Black women's self-definitions is distinctive. Self is not defined as the increased autonomy gained by separating oneself from others. Instead, self is found in the context of family and community—as Paule Marshall describes it, "the ability to recognize one's continuity with the larger community" (Washington 1984, 159). By being accountable to others, African-American women develop more fully human, less objectified selves. Sonia Sanchez points to this version of self by stating, "we must move past always focusing on the 'personal self' because there's a larger self. There's a 'self' of black people" (Tate 1983, 134). Rather than defining self in opposition to others, the connectedness among individuals provides Black women deeper, more meaningful self-definitions.[6]

This journey toward self-definition has political significance. As Mary Helen Washington observes, Black women who struggle to "forge an identity larger than the one society would force upon them … are aware and conscious, and that very consciousness is potent" (1980, xv). Identity is not the goal but rather the point of departure in the process of self-definition. In this process Black women journey toward an understanding of how our personal lives have been fundamentally shaped by interlocking systems of race, gender, and class oppression. Peaches's statement, "I'm awfully bitter these days because my parents were slaves," illustrates this transformation.

The journey toward self-definition offers a powerful challenge to the externally defined, controlling images of African-American women. Replacing negative images with positive ones can be equally problematic if the function of stereotypes as controlling images remains unrecognized. John Gwaltney's (1980) interview with Nancy White, a 73-year-old Black woman, suggests that ordinary Black women can be acutely aware of the power of these controlling images. To Nancy White the difference between the controlling images applied to African-American and white women are those of degree, not of kind:

> My mother used to say that the black woman is the white man's mule and the white woman is his dog. Now, she said that to say this: we do the heavy work and get beat whether we do it well or not. But the white woman is closer to the

master and he pats them on the head and lets them sleep in the house, but he ain't gon' treat neither one like he was dealing with a person, (p. 148)

Although both groups are objectified, albeit in different ways, the function of the images is to dehumanize and control both groups. Seen in this light, it makes little sense in the long run for Black women to exchange one set of controlling images for another even if positive stereotypes bring better treatment in the short run.

The insistence on Black female self-definition reframes the entire dialogue from one of protesting the technical accuracy of an image—namely, refuting the Black matriarchy thesis—to one stressing the power dynamics underlying the very process of definition itself. By insisting on self-definition, Black women question not only what has been said about African-American women but the credibility and the intentions of those possessing the power to define. When Black women define ourselves, we clearly reject the assumption that those in positions granting them the authority to interpret our reality are entitled to do so. Regardless of the actual content of Black women's self-definitions, the act of insisting on Black female self-definition validates Black women's power as human subjects.

References

Cannon, Katie G. 1988. Black Womanist Ethics. Atlanta: Scholars Press.

Christian, Barbara. 1985. Black Feminist Criticism, Perspectives on Black Women Writers. New York: Pergamon.

Davis, Angela Y. 1989. Women, Culture, and Politics. New York: Random House.

Evans, Sara. 1979. Personal Politics. New York: Vintage.

Giovanni, Nikki. 1971. Gemini. New York: Penguin.

Gwaltney, John Langston. 1980. Drylongso, A Self-Portrait of Black America. New York: Vintage.

Harris, Trudier. 1988. Black Pearls: Blues Queens of the 1920s. New Brunswick, NJ: Rutgers University Press.

Lorde, Audre. 1984. Sister Outsider. Trumansberg, NY: Crossing Press.

O'Neale, Sondra. 1986. "Inhibiting Midwives, Usurping Creators: The Struggling Emergence of Black Women in American Fiction." In Feminist Studies/Critical Studies, ed. Teresa de Lauretis, 139–56. Bloomington: Indiana University Press.

Simone, Nina. 1985. Backlash. Portugal: Movieplay Portuguesa Recording.

Tate, Claudia, ed. 1983. Black Women Writers at Work. New York: Continuum Publishing.

Washington, Mary Helen, ed. 1980. Midnight Birds. Garden City, NY: Anchor.

——— . 1984. "I Sign My Mother's Name: Alice Walker, Dorothy West and Paule Marshall." In Mothering the Mind: Twelve Studies of Writers and Their Silent Partners, ed. Ruth Perry and Martine Watson Broronley, 143–63. New York: Holmes & Meier.

Williams, Sherley A. 1979. "The Blues Roots of Afro-American Poetry." In Chant of Saints: A Gathering of Afro-American Literature, Art and Scholarship, ed. Michael S. Harper and Robert B. Steptoe, 123–35. Urbana: University of Illinois Press.

....

Planned Parenthood v. Casey

Justice Antonin Scalia laments in his dissent of *Planned Parenthood v. Casey*, "There is no liberty in a jurisprudence of doubt." The doubt he refers to is the confusing departure from the trimester framework established by the Supreme Court earlier in the *Roe v. Wade* decision. While some found clarity in that decision for women who sought reproductive rights in the first trimester, following the decision state and local agencies, as well as politicians and pundits, made efforts to both improve and restrict access to medical abortion consultations in the second and third trimesters. Note how Justice Sandra Day O'Connor draws a line for future litigation and for state policy that provides a framework for deciding what would be an "unreasonable burden" to prevent women from exercising their reproductive rights. How would you define *burden*? Is this framework helpful for other constitutional controversies that involve a weighing of competing rights?

....

from

Planned Parenthood of Southeastern Pa. v. Casey

505 U.S. 833. June 29, 1992.[3]

Liberty finds no refuge in a jurisprudence of doubt.

---

3   Opinion by Justice O'Connor, Selections from Planned Parenthood of Southeastern Pa. v. Casey 505 U.S. 833 (1992), pp. 844–847, 850, 874. Copyright in the Public Domain.

Yet 19 years after our holding that the Constitution protects a woman's right to terminate her pregnancy in its early stages, *Roe v. Wade*, 410 U.S. 113 (1973), that definition of liberty is still questioned. Joining the respondents as *amicus curiae*, the United States, as it has done in five other cases in the last decade, again asks us to overrule *Roe*. At issue in these cases are five provisions of the Pennsylvania Abortion Control Act of 1982 as amended in 1988 and 1989. 18 Pa. Cons. Stat. §§ 3203–3220 (1990). Relevant portions of the Act are set forth in the appendix. *Infra*, at 60. The Act requires that a woman seeking an abortion give her informed consent prior to the abortion procedure, and specifies that she be provided with certain information at least 24 hours before the abortion is performed. § 3205. For a minor to obtain an abortion, the Act requires the informed consent of one of her parents, but provides for a judicial bypass option if the minor does not wish to or cannot obtain a parent's consent. § 3206. Another provision of the Act requires that, unless certain exceptions apply, a married woman seeking an abortion must sign a statement indicating that she has notified her husband of her intended abortion. § 3209. The Act exempts compliance with these three requirements in the event of a "medical emergency," which is defined in § 3203 of the Act. See §§ 3203, 3205(a), 3206(a), 3209(c). In addition to the above provisions regulating the performance of abortions, the Act imposes certain reporting requirements on facilities that provide abortion services. §§ 3207(b), 3214(a), 3214(f).

After considering the fundamental constitutional questions resolved by *Roe*, principles of institutional integrity, and the rule of stare decisis, we are led to conclude this: the essential holding of *Roe v. Wade* should be retained and once again reaffirmed.

It must be stated at the outset and with clarity that *Roe's* essential holding, the holding we reaffirm, has three parts. First is a recognition of the right of the woman to choose to have an abortion before viability and to obtain it without undue interference from the State. Before viability, the State's interests are not strong enough to support a prohibition of abortion or the imposition of a substantial obstacle to the woman's effective right to elect the procedure. Second is a confirmation of the State's power to restrict abortions after fetal viability, if the law contains exceptions for pregnancies which endanger a woman's life or health. And third is the principle that the State has legitimate interests from the outset of the pregnancy in protecting the health of the woman and the life of the fetus that may become a child. These principles do not contradict one another; and we adhere to each.

Constitutional protection of the woman's decision to terminate her pregnancy derives from the Due Process Clause of the Fourteenth Amendment. It declares that no State shall "deprive any person of life, liberty, or property, without due process of law." The controlling word in the case before us is "liberty." Although a literal reading of the Clause might suggest that it governs only the procedures by which a State may deprive persons of liberty, for at least 105 years, at least since *Mugler v. Kansas*, 123 U.S. 623, 660–661 (1887), the Clause has been understood to contain a substantive component as well, one "barring certain government actions regardless of the fairness of the procedures used to implement them." *Daniels v. Williams*, 474 U.S. 327, 331 (1986). As Justice Brandeis (joined by Justice Holmes) observed, "[d]espite arguments to the contrary which had seemed to me persuasive, it is settled that the due process clause of the Fourteenth Amendment applies to matters of substantive law as well as to matters of procedure. Thus all fundamental rights comprised within the term liberty are protected by the Federal Constitution from invasion by the States." *Whitney v. California*, 274 U.S. 357, 373 (1927) (Brandeis, J., concurring). "[T]he guaranties of due process, though having their roots in Magna Carta's '*per legem terrae*' and considered as procedural safeguards 'against executive usurpation and tyranny,' have in this country 'become bulwarks also against arbitrary legislation.'" *Poe v. Ullman*, 367 U.S. 497, 541 (1961) (Harlan, J., dissenting from dismissal on jurisdictional grounds) (quoting *Hurtado v. California*, 110 U.S. 516, 532 (1884)).

Men and women of good conscience can disagree, and we suppose some always shall disagree, about the profound moral and spiritual implications of terminating a pregnancy, even in its earliest stage. Some of us as individuals find abortion offensive to our most basic principles of morality, but that cannot control our decision. Our obligation is to define the liberty of all, not to mandate our own moral code. The underlying constitutional issue is whether the State can resolve these philosophic questions in such a definitive way that a woman lacks all choice in the matter, except perhaps in those rare circumstances in which the pregnancy is itself a danger to her own life or health, or is the result of rape or incest.

Numerous forms of state regulation might have the incidental effect of increasing the cost or decreasing the availability of medical care, whether for abortion or any other medical procedure. The fact that a law which serves a valid purpose, one not designed to strike at the right itself, has the incidental effect of making it more difficult or more expensive to procure an abortion cannot be enough to invalidate it. Only where state regulation imposes an undue burden on a woman's ability to make this decision does the power of the State reach into the heart of the liberty protected by the Due Process Clause. See *Hodgson v. Minnesota*, 497 U.S. 417, 458–459 (1990) (O'Connor, J., concurring in part and concurring in judgment in part); *Ohio v. Akron Center for Reproductive Health*, 497 U.S. 502.

....

The Modern Clerkship: Ginsburg

In this reading we present an insider's view of a Supreme Court Justice often considered as a relative outsider to the other members of the court and in historical terms. Justice Ruth Bader Ginsburg has been a relentless advocate for a living Constitution and for women's equality. It is interesting to observe how she organizes this civic work as a model for individual and group agency. As the Supreme Court embraces political and social conflicts, how these cases are managed influences how the Supreme Court will interpret and frame the binding legal decision for future courts, as well as how we understand the parameters of the debates. As you read through the responsibilities of judicial clerks, think of how these duties also create opportunities. In what areas can change be most successful at the country's highest court?

···

from

The Modern Clerkship: Justice Ruth Bader Ginsburg and Her Law Clerks

In Chambers: Stories of Supreme Court Law Clerks and Their Justices. University of Virginia Press, 2012. 392–398.[4]

Todd C. Peppers and Artemus Ward

The Selection of the Ginsburg Law Clerks

Like most current justices, Justice Ginsburg herself does not review the hundreds of applications of prospective law clerks. Instead, she relies upon the "good judgment" of Columbia Law School dean David Schizer, himself a former Ginsburg law clerk, to fill one of the clerkship slots. "He will not bother me with five or six applications, but he will recommend one person—usually someone who has completed a clerkship." Regarding her selection criteria, Justice Ginsburg stated that "I don't want the brightest person in the graduating class; I want someone who has had a year of a clerkship." Justice Ginsburg will then meet with Dean Schizer's recommended applicant before making a hiring decision.[2]

For the remaining clerkship slots, Justice Ginsburg states that she "relies mostly on certain Court of Appeals judges for giving me an appraisal [of applicants]." Justice Ginsburg conceded that recommendations are not always reliable since some judges "exaggerate" the abilities of their clerks, but she added that there are other federal appeals court judges—such as William A. Fletcher of the United States Court of Appeals for the Ninth Circuit and David S. Tatel of the United States Court of Appeals for the District of Columbia Circuit—in whose recommendations she is confident.[3] Relying upon "feeder court judges" for law clerks is a well-established practice followed by all members of the present Court, and studies have suggested that the justices depend on federal appeals court judges to guarantee both the competence and ideological compatibility of their clerks.[4]

---

4   Todd C. Peppers and Artemus Ward, "The Modern Clerkship: Justice Ruth Bader Ginsburg and Her Law Clerks," *In Chambers: Stories of Supreme Court Law Clerks and Their Justices*, pp. 392–398. Copyright © 2012 by University of Virginia Press. Reprinted with permission.

Until his death in 2010, Justice Ginsburg had her "in-house reader" (namely, her late husband and Georgetown law professor Martin Ginsburg) review the finalists' writing samples. Professor Ginsburg was familiar with the writing style that Justice Ginsburg prefers, and he tried to select those candidates who would be "someone that would be easy for me to deal with," stated the justice. "Some young lawyers tend to be more elaborate, and my husband will spot them." According to an interview with Professor Ginsburg, he looked for applicants who evidenced "[c]lean writing and non-complexity. I do not look for obvious consistency with RBG's writing, but I do hope for a clue whether the student likely will absorb and reflect RBG's writing."

Since the late 1960s, a federal appeals court clerkship has become a de facto requirement for a Supreme Court clerkship—a practice Justice Ginsburg herself follows. When asked why she prefers applicants with prior clerkship experience, Justice Ginsburg replied that it provides her with an "an appraisal of the applicant. Explained the justice: "A number of law clerks look very good on paper, but they didn't work out—mainly because they are terrific issue spotters, but they are lacking in a certain judgment and common sense. [This is a deficient that you really can't spot] just from their performance in law school."

Justice Ginsburg interviews the finalists, but she neither has a standard set of questions to ask nor routinely poses substantive questions about the law. "I don't quiz them to see how well prepared they are," stated the justice. "Many of them are [well prepared], so they try to work in 'your opinion in such-and-such.'" For the justice, the interview is designed to get to know the applicant. "I interview so few that I will have certain questions in my own mind about the person's background."

Former Ginsburg law clerk Kate Andrias (October term 2006) keenly remembers her interview with the justice, which she describes as a "wonderful experience."

Even if I hadn't been hired, however, I would have treasured the chance to speak with the Justice for an extended period of time. We discussed a range of topics, including our shared interest in France (where my husband grew up and where her daughter spends a significant amount of time); her experiences as a litigator and as a woman in the legal profession; articles I had published and work I had done as a researcher for a professor; and a few recent cases of the Court. She did not ask specific legal questions, but I do recall discussing substantive legal issues during the conversation.

When asked if there is a particular type of applicant personality toward which she gravitates, Justice Ginsburg stated, "number one, they have to show respect for my secretaries." She further explained:

> There was one law clerk applicant who came to interview with me—top rating at Harvard—who treated my secretaries with disdain. As if they were just minions. So that is one very important thing—how you deal with my secretaries. They are not hired help. As I tell my clerks, "if push came to shove, I could do your work—but I can't do without my secretaries."

Concluded Justice Ginsburg: "I try to avoid the arrogant type."

In recent years, the Supreme Court justices have been criticized for a lack of diversity in their clerkship hiring.[5] While Justice Ginsburg hires more female and minority candidates than other justices, she still selects her clerks from a small handful of elite law schools (the majority of her clerks come from Columbia, Yale, or Harvard). Justice Ginsburg conceded that she does not make "a deliberate attempt" to pick applicants from law schools not traditionally represented in the law clerk corps, but the justice made it equally clear that a degree from a lesser law school does not disqualify a candidate—a fact evident in a few of her law clerks' educational backgrounds.[6]

As noted above, social scientists and legal scholars have written about the ideological harmony between modern justices and their clerks—a consistent pattern that suggests that the justices are using an ideological litmus test to pick their clerks. I asked Justice Ginsburg if she prefers to have clerks from across the ideological spectrum. She replied that she doesn't try to get such a mixture of preferences, but that "it sometimes happens." Former law clerks dismiss the suggestion that the justice applies an ideological litmus test, and it does appear that she is not deterred when the applications of potential law clerks manifest evidence of more conservative preferences, such as membership in the Federalist Society. "One of my best clerks was a Federalist Society member," observed the justice.

Given the 2009 confirmation hearings of Justice Sonia Sotomayor, I asked Justice Ginsburg if she herself started thinking about how she would select and use her law clerks during her Supreme Court confirmation hearings. "There really wasn't a serious question about my getting confirmed, because there was a bipartisan spirit prevailing and I was the beneficiary of their [Congress's] rebounding from what happened to Justice Thomas," remarked the justice. "So my hearings were rather boring, and there wasn't much doubt that I was going to be confirmed. So I started—after I got done filing the endless paperwork and forms and Senate questionnaire—I did think about law clerks."

While some justices have a clerk serve a second year as a "senior" or supervisory clerk, Justice Ginsburg traditionally hires clerks for one term. "During my first year here I had somebody for two years," recalled the justice, "but it didn't work out and I decided I wasn't going to do that anymore." The firm, one-year rule has the practical effect of guaranteeing that poor personality matches are rectified yearly. "Sometimes you will have someone you love and wish that the person could stay forever, but sometimes you are happy [to see them go]." As for why permanent clerks haven't caught on at the Supreme Court (as they have in the lower federal courts), Justice Ginsburg replied that a Supreme Court clerkship is "very intense. It's like a treadmill that gets faster and faster, and I think that you reach a burnout point."

The Job Duties of the Ginsburg Law Clerks

The day-to-day clerkship practices adopted by Justice Ginsburg are based, at least in part, on the previous traditions of her predecessor, Associate Justice Byron White. "I had very good counsel," observed Justice Ginsburg. "It was Justice White who gave me his chambers manual, the operating procedures that he had written for his chambers early on and gave it over to his law clerks." The chambers manual was later revised by the Ginsburg clerks. The tradition of passing down the chambers manual to the newest member of the Court has been perpetuated by Justice Ginsburg. "The day that Sonia [Sotomayor] was sworn in, I was away ... but I had delivered to her that chambers manual."

The job duties of the Ginsburg law clerks fall into three main categories: reviewing cert petitions, preparing bench memoranda, and writing opinion drafts. The "pooling" of cert petitions for review by the law clerks of the justices is a fairly new institutional practice,[7] and like all current justices save Samuel Alito, Justice Ginsburg is a member of the cert pool. Justice Ginsburg stated that—in the beginning of her tenure—it "certainly wasn't much of a decision" to become a member of the cert pool. "So much was new, and I didn't need one thing more."

Justice Ginsburg, however, also requires her law clerks to review the cert pool memos, either annotating them in the upper left-hand corner or preparing a new cover memo. When asked why she has adopted a second layer of review, the justice explained that the law clerks who write pool memoranda are writing for the entire Court, and that her law clerks—who are reviewing the cert pool memos—are writing *just* for her and her particular interests. In other words, "the trouble with some law clerks [in the cert pool] is that they don't appreciate that they are writing for the Court rather than for their justice."

The justice categorically rejected the argument that the cert pool results in the justices abdicating their responsibility of "deciding to decide." In an interview given shortly after her confirmation to the Court, Justice Ginsburg bluntly stated: "Some people outside the court seem to think the cert. pool makes it all a piece of cake—that the justices simply read and follow what the law clerks recommend … [b]ut, to quote Sportin' Life, 'It ain't necessarily so.'"[8]

When asked if she ever feared that law clerks in other chambers were playing fast and loose with the cert memoranda in order to achieve a certain result, Justice Ginsburg quickly replied, "Not for grants." A few former Ginsburg law clerks have suggested that their review of the cert pool memos does ferret out mediocrity as well as clumsy efforts at manipulation, adding that clerks who tried to use the cert pool process to improperly influence other chambers were quickly identified and their future memos more closely scrutinized.[9]

Justice Ginsburg's clerks prepare bench memoranda in some—but not all—cases. "The cases in the October sitting are one-issue cases and easy to grasp," the justice explained. "I don't need bench memos in those cases." Justice Ginsburg asks her clerks to prepare bench memoranda in the more complex cases. "Their job is to give me a road map through the case, and then I can read the briefs. They also tell me which of the green briefs [the amicus curiae briefs] I can skip." While it is not obligatory in the bench memos, the law clerks can also suggest questions to ask at oral argument. Finally, the clerks inevitably give a recommended disposition on the merits of the case. "They want to give it to me, and they always do, but it's not important."

Justice Ginsburg quickly dismissed my suggestion that the bench memoranda might provide a conduit through which law clerks exercise influence, pointing out that her memoranda are designed to merely provide guidance to the court file and to summarize facts. In sum, the bench memoranda are designed "to be a road map to everything that I have to read [in the case] and to bring the case to the front of my mind just before oral argument."

Former Ginsburg clerks are equally skeptical that, at least in the Ginsburg chambers, the bench memo holds much sway over the justice's decision making. Writes law clerk Jay Wexler (October term 1998): "Some Justices discuss the cases intensely with their clerks; RBG tended to do relatively little of that (clerks generally refer to the Justices by their initials). In fact, one of the great things about my job was that, being generally brilliant and having been on the bench for twenty years already, RBG basically knew everything already and could make up her mind about a case without much help from her clerks at all. This made the job fairly easy. Some Ginsburg clerks have been known to work sixteen hour days, but I honestly can't imagine what they spent their time doing."[10]

Of course, the most controversial aspect of the modern Supreme Court clerkship involves the role of law clerks in drafting opinions. Presently, all justices routinely have their clerks prepare the first drafts of majority, concurring, and dissenting opinions (recently retired justice John Paul Stevens was the only member of the Roberts Court who followed the now-outdated practice of preparing his own opinion drafts). Once Justice Ginsburg is assigned to write a majority opinion, she adheres to the following process:

> I read over everything … I start with the opinion below, I reread the briefs, the bench memo—if I had one—and then I write the opening. It will be any where from one to three paragraphs. It's kind of a press release, and it will tell you what the issue was and how it was resolved. After the opening, I will make a detailed outline of how I think the opinion should go. I give that outline to the law clerk. Sometimes, to my delight, they will give me a draft that I can make my own version through heavy editing, but I don't have to redo it. I'd say it's a good year if I have two law clerks that have that skill. In most cases, what they do is always valuable to me—sometimes I see that my organization was not right and should be done another way. So their draft is always of use to me, but in most cases I can't simply take it over.

Softly laughing, Justice Ginsburg added that "mostly, I would like to do all of my own work so I could write all my opinions myself, but there is just not enough time to do that."

As the Ginsburg clerks begin the opinion-drafting process, they undoubtedly keep in mind what former Ginsburg law clerk David Schizer (October term 1994) calls the "chamber motto"—"Get it right and keep it tight." Getting an opinion "right" means not only a correct analysis of the law, but duly acknowledging and analyzing opposing points of view. Explains Schizer: law clerks are instructed to "[b]e scrupulously fair to counter-arguments—or, as the Justice puts it, 'don't sweep the other side's chess pieces off the table.'"[11]

Moreover, a "right and tight" opinion is one that Justice Ginsburg described as "spare" and plainly written, limited to "the essentials" and devoid of "decorations and deviations" as well as arcane Latin phrases. Justice Ginsburg joked that she has worked on her colleagues to stop using Latin phrases in their opinions. "We do not say 'collateral estoppel' or 'res judicata'; we say 'claim preclusion' and 'issue preclusion.' So if I've left a mark on the Court, it's the change [in opinion writing] to plain language."

When asked why she has pushed for plainer language, Justice Ginsburg spoke of the dangers of "jargon" used in articles across different disciplines (such as law or sociology) and the impact of said jargon on the reader. "I don't fool myself into thinking that I can write for a layman, but at least I can write for a Linda Greenhouse or for my dear friend Nina Totenberg, who is not a lawyer."

Former Ginsburg appeals court clerk David Post explains that, for the justice, "[l]anguage matters more than you can imagine … I've seen her agonize over individual words many times. Not terms of art, but adjectives." Adds Post: "It's very important to her to get every word to say exactly what she wants it to say, with all the connotations she wants."[12] His comments are echoed by former Supreme Court clerk Andrias, who observes: "Justice Ginsburg has a distinct writing style. As the year went on, we became increasingly familiar with it and tried to hew closely to it. She likes precise and direct writing; does not like lengthy introductory clauses; prefers some words to others; and does not like excessive footnotes. I recall that after another clerk and I completed our first writing assignment for her—a draft of an introduction to a book—she sat down with us and went over our draft line by line to explain her edits and her writing style."

The care and attention paid to the substance and style of a draft opinion does not end when the law clerk assigned to the case finishes the draft; after said clerk completes a draft, it is reviewed by the other clerks before it is given to Justice Ginsburg—a procedure suggested to her by Justice Sandra Day O'Connor after Justice Ginsburg had been on the Supreme Court bench for three years. "Every clerk will have a copy of my outline," stated Justice Ginsburg, "and they review each other's work" before submitting to the justice.

As with the bench memoranda, former Ginsburg law clerks reject the claims that law clerks wield influence over crafting constitutional law. Referring to the role of law clerks in drafting opinions as "not that big a deal," former clerk Wexler writes that "the boss would give us a detailed outline to work from and then, once we turned in our drafts, totally rewrite them. The best you could really hope for as a clerk is to get a little pet phrase or goofy word or other quirky something-or-other into the final opinion." As an example of a "quirky something-or-other," Wexler adds (tongue in cheek): "[T]here may or may not be one Ginsburg opinion from our term which, when read backwards, will summon the demon Beelzebub from the seventh level of hell to earth where he will horribly murder the entire human race."[13]

In discussing opinion writing with the justice, I shared former Hugo Black law clerk John P. Frank's lament that the color and distinctiveness of judicial opinions are drained away when law clerks get involved in the drafting process.[14] Justice Ginsburg agreed in part, with the caveat that "it depends on the justice. I can always tell a Scalia opinion, even if there is no name on it—he will make each opinion genuinely his own. His spicy style is not something that is a function of a clerk."[15]

Notes

The information in this essay is primarily based on my August 14, 2009, interview with Associate Justice Ruth Bader Ginsburg. Additional information comes from written correspondence with Georgetown law professor Martin D. Ginsburg and for- mer Ginsburg law clerks Kate A ndrias, Heather Elliott, Goodwin Liu, and Deborah Merritt.

2. Justice Ginsburg added that she had a similar arrangement with former Harvard Law School dean Elena Kagan.

3. Both Fletcher and Tatel were appointed to the federal bench by President Bill Clinton, with Judge Tatel replacing Justice Ginsburg upon her nomination to the Supreme Court.

4. William E. Nelson, Harvey R ishikof, I. Scott Messinger, and Michael Jo, "The Liberal Tradition of the Supreme Court Clerkship: Its R ise, Fall, and Reincarnation?" *Vanderbilt Law Review* 62, no. 6 (2009): 1749–1814; Corey A. Ditslear and Lawrence Baum, "Selection of Law Clerks and Polarization in the U.S. Supreme Court," *Journal of Politics* 63, no. 3 (2001): 869–85.

5. See Tony Mauro, "Corps of Clerks Lacking in Diversity," *USA Today*, March 13, 1998; Mauro, "Only 1 New High Court Clerk Is a Minority," *USA Today*, September 10, 1998.

6. At least one on occasion, the justice has demonstrated a willingness to look for diversity regarding the age of her clerks. Typically, the modern Supreme Court law clerk arrives at the Supreme Court only a year or two removed from law school. During October term 1996, however, one of the justice's law clerks was W. William Hodes, a law professor in his early fifties who had once taken a class from the justice when she taught at Rutgers Law School. See Laurie Asseo, "Former Ginsburg Student Becomes Her Law Clerk," *Salt Lake City Deseret News*, June 8, 1996.

7. For a thorough discussion on the creation of the cert pool, see Artemus Ward and David L. Weiden, *Sorcerers' Apprentices: 100 Years of Law Clerks at the United States Supreme Court* (New York: New York University Press, 2006), 117–24.

8. Associated Press, "Ginsburg: Court Agenda Not Determined by Clerks," January 3, 1994.

9. Todd C. Peppers, *Courtiers of the Marble Palace: The Rise and Influence of the Supreme Court Law Clerk* (Stanford, Calif.: Stanford University Press, 2006), 198–99.

10. Jay Wexler, "Clerkin' for R BG." http://holyhullabaloos.typepad.com/files/clerkin2.pdf.

11. David Schizer, "Former Law Clerks to Justice Ginsburg Reminisce," Columbia Law School website, n.d., http://www.law.columbia.edu/law_school/communications/reports/winter2004/clerks.

12. David Post, quoted in Jeffrey Rosen, "The New Look of Liberalism on the Court," *New York Times Magazine*, October 5, 1997.

13. Wexler, "Clerkin' for R BG."

14. In discussing the role of Chief Justice Fred Vinson's law clerks in drafting Supreme Court opinions, John Frank argued that the practical result was that said opinions suffered from a lack of judicial personality, such as "the Holmes epigram, theBlack way with facts, the Frankfurter vocabulary, the Brandeis footnote, the Stone

pragmatism." John P. Frank, "Fred Vinson and the Chief Justiceship," *University of Chicago Law Review* 21, no. 1 (Autumn 1954): 212–46, at 224.

15. For an interesting take on the effect that law clerks have on the language of Supreme Court opinions, see Paul J. Wahlbeck, James F. Spriggs II, and Lee Sigelman, "Ghostwriters on the Court? A Stylistic A nalysis of U.S. Supreme Court Opinion Drafts," *American Politics Research* 30, no. 2 (2002): 166–92.

· ·

In Those Years

We have thus far presented scenes of civic identity and agency as they relate to legal and governmental systems. We imagine a framework for change that allows individuals and groups to self-identify, explore different civic identities in relationship with one another, and recognize agency for change through this dialogue. We have also made a consistent effort to present a variety of sources and ways of making meaning throughout this text. We now offer a short but impactful poem that reminds us of the objective external realities happening all around us. From war and violence to the general problem of crime and deviance in a free society, we want to transition to the urgent task of sober reflection and setting out a plan for change. In Those Years, we see the relationship between "I" and "we" in the long track of history.

....

from

In Those Years

Dark Fields of the Republic: Poems 1991–1995.
W.W. Norton & Company, Inc., 1995. 4.[5]

Adrienne Rich

In Those Years

In those years, people will say, we lost track
of the meaning of *we*, of *you*
we found ourselves
reduced to *I*
and the whole thing became
silly, ironic, terrible:
we were trying to live a personal life and, yes, that was the only life
we could bear witness to

But the great dark birds of history screamed and plunged
into our personal weather
They were headed somewhere else but their beaks and pinions drove
along the shore, through the rags of fog
where we stood, saying *I*

....

DISCUSSION QUESTIONS

1. What is an example of an injustice in your own life or in the life of someone you know and care about?
2. What is an injustice in your community?
3. What is an injustice in the country?

---

[5]   Adrienne Rich, "In Those Years," *Dark Fields of the Republic*, p. 4. Copyright © 1995 by W. W. Norton & Company, Inc. Reprinted with permission.

Declaration of Independence v. Lincoln's Portrait: In Reflection

As we conclude this section on critical civic challenges, we want to review two historical epics of civic change: the Declaration of Independence and the advocacy of President Abraham Lincoln. As the notion for equality of political power was first articulated against the totalitarianism of an expanding imperial Britain, we invite you to read the Declaration out loud and consider its practical importance today. In our studies, we have found that the proclamations made by the early American revolutionaries were as different from each other as they are today on many of the same issues, but a common dedication of life, fortune, and sacred honor created a space for respectful dialogue around the most important questions of life, liberty, and the pursuit of happiness. Contrast this reading to the artfully crafted rendition of Lincoln and we get a sense of the sober mind for social change through revolutionary efforts. From a simple definition of *democratic thinking* emerges a complex world of intercultural exchanges about what it means to be free in a constitutional representative democracy. No doubt these reminders of historical political struggle are needed today as much, if not more, than in those times of strife and discord.

....

from

IN CONGRESS

July 4, 1776.

The unanimous Declaration of the thirteen united States of America,

When in the Course of human events, it becomes necessary for one people to dissolve the political bands which have connected them with another, and to assume among the powers of the earth, the separate and equal station to which the Laws of Nature and of Nature's God entitle them, a decent respect to the opinions of mankind requires that they should declare the causes which impel them to the separation.

And for the support of this Declaration, with a firm reliance on the protection of divine Providence, we mutually pledge to each other our Lives, our Fortunes and our sacred Honor.

....

··

from

Copland's 'Lincoln Portrait'

National Public Radio, 2004.[6]

Aaron Copland (Fred Child, ed.)

"Fellow citizens, we cannot escape history."

That is what he said. That is what Abraham Lincoln said.

"Fellow citizens, we cannot escape history. We of this congress and this administration will be remembered in spite of ourselves. No personal significance or insignificance can spare one or another of us. The fiery trial through which we pass will light us down in honor or dishonor to the latest generation. We, even we here, hold the power and bear the responsibility." [Annual Message to Congress, December 1, 1862]

He was born in Kentucky, raised in Indiana, and lived in Illinois. And this is what he said. This is what Abe Lincoln said.

"The dogmas of the quiet past are inadequate to the stormy present. The occasion is piled high with difficulty and we must rise with the occasion. As our case is new, so we must think anew and act anew. We must disenthrall ourselves and then we will save our country." [Annual Message to Congress, December 1, 1862]

When standing erect he was six feet four inches tall, and this is what he said.

He said: "It is the eternal struggle between two principles, right and wrong, throughout the world. It is the same spirit that says 'you toil and work and earn bread, and I'll eat it.' No matter in what shape it comes, whether from the mouth of a king who seeks to bestride the people of his own nation, and live by the fruit of their labor, or from one race of men as an apology for enslaving another race, it is the same tyrannical principle." [Lincoln-Douglas debates, 15 October 1858]

Lincoln was a quiet man. Abe Lincoln was a quiet and a melancholy man. But when he spoke of democracy, this is what he said.

---

6   Aaron Copland; ed. Fred Child, "Lincoln Portrait," NPR Books. Commentary Copyright © 2004 by National Public Radio (NPR).

He said: "As I would not be a slave, so I would not be a master. This expresses my idea of democracy. Whatever differs from this, to the extent of the difference, is no democracy."

Abraham Lincoln, sixteenth president of these United States, is everlasting in the memory of his countrymen. For on the battleground at Gettysburg, this is what he said:

He said: "That from these honored dead we take increased devotion to that cause for which they gave the last full measure of devotion. That we here highly resolve that these dead shall not have died in vain. That this nation under God shall have a new birth of freedom and that government of the people, by the people, and for the people shall not perish from the earth."

....

In reflection:

Look back at your response to what skills you have that you could use to make a difference. In small groups, make a list of actions needed to overcome one of the challenges you identified in the discussion questions.

Sharing Your Inquiry Question Responses

Democratic processes are transparent and accountable. Consider using digital or nondigital portfolios to share your responses with others. Your documentation process provides a helpful tool for other educators and learners and can also be used to showcase some of your best work. Civic agency can be best evidenced through democratic action with others.

Civic Advocacy through Action Research in the Community

I n this final section, we provide multiple theoretical frameworks that can be used to conduct action research in any community. We first examine how the Constitution seeks to organize political and social power. We then consider more recent understanding of the human decision-making process, particularly as it applies to organizations and change. We then discuss the so-called separation of powers theory and offer a road map for nongovernmental and governmental organizational change. The final readings bring the focus back onto civic identity and agency from the points of view of class, war, diversity, new technology, protest, and finally, competing identities. These readings are intended to be read as a sequence leading into the final reflection. Feel free to interrupt the readings with your own discussion questions or take on a framework to apply to a final class project or essay.

INQUIRY QUESTION

It is our goal that by this point your inquiry question would be particular to the group of learners working with you as co-researchers. Thus, one possible direction would be to co-create an inquiry question that extends beyond the semester, program, or even major.

Marbury v. Madison

Chief Justice John Marshall is notorious for articulating the Supreme Court's domain over the interpretation of the Constitution. As the decision outlines the vision of a constitutional system of government, examine the validity of the claims today.

....

from

Marbury v. Madison

5 U.S. 137, 1803.[1]

"The Government of the United States has been emphatically termed a government of laws, and not of men. It will certainly cease to deserve this high appellation if the laws furnish no remedy for the violation of a vested legal right (163).

The question whether an act repugnant to the Constitution can become the law of the land is a question deeply interesting to the United States, but, happily, not of an intricacy proportioned to its interest. It seems only necessary to recognize certain principles, supposed to have been long and well established, to decide it.

That the people have an original right to establish for their future government such principles as, in their opinion, shall most conduce to their own happiness is the basis on which the whole American fabric has been erected. The exercise of this original right is a very great exertion; nor can it nor ought it to be frequently repeated. The principles, therefore, so established are deemed fundamental. And as the authority from which they proceed, is supreme, and can seldom act, they are designed to be permanent.

---

1   Chief Justice Marshall, Selections from Marbury v. Madison, pp. 163–180. Copyright in the Public Domain.

This original and supreme will organizes the government and assigns to different departments their respective powers. It may either stop here or establish certain limits not to be transcended by those departments.

The Government of the United States is of the latter description. The powers of the Legislature are defined and limited; and that those limits may not be mistaken or forgotten, the Constitution is written. To what purpose are powers limited, and to what purpose is that limitation committed to writing, if these limits may at any time be passed by those intended to be restrained? The distinction between a government with limited and unlimited powers is abolished if those limits do not confine the persons on whom they are imposed, and if acts prohibited and acts allowed are of equal obligation. It is a proposition too plain to be contested that the Constitution controls any legislative act repugnant to it, or that the Legislature may alter the Constitution by an ordinary act.

Between these alternatives there is no middle ground. The Constitution is either a superior, paramount law, unchangeable by ordinary means, or it is on a level with ordinary legislative acts, and, like other acts, is alterable when the legislature shall please to alter it.

If the former part of the alternative be true, then a legislative act contrary to the Constitution is not law; if the latter part be true, then written Constitutions are absurd attempts on the part of the people to limit a power in its own nature illimitable.

Certainly all those who have framed written Constitutions contemplate them as forming the fundamental and paramount law of the nation, and consequently the theory of every such government must be that an act of the Legislature repugnant to the Constitution is void.

This theory is essentially attached to a written Constitution, and is consequently to be considered by this Court as one of the fundamental principles of our society. It is not, therefore, to be lost sight of in the further consideration of this subject.

If an act of the Legislature repugnant to the Constitution is void, does it, notwithstanding its invalidity, bind the Courts and oblige them to give it effect? Or, in other words, though it be not law, does it constitute a rule as operative as if it was a law? This would be to overthrow in fact what was established in theory, and would seem, at first view, an absurdity too gross to be insisted on. It shall, however, receive a more attentive consideration.

It is emphatically the province and duty of the Judicial Department to say what the law is. Those who apply the rule to particular cases must, of necessity, expound and interpret that rule. If two laws conflict with each other, the Courts must decide on the operation of each.

So, if a law be in opposition to the Constitution, if both the law and the Constitution apply to a particular case, so that the Court must either decide that case conformably to the law, disregarding the Constitution, or conformably to the Constitution, disregarding the law, the Court must determine which of these conflicting rules governs the case. This is of the very essence of judicial duty.

If, then, the Courts are to regard the Constitution, and the Constitution is superior to any ordinary act of the Legislature, the Constitution, and not such ordinary act, must govern the case to which they both apply.

Those, then, who controvert the principle that the Constitution is to be considered in court as a paramount law are reduced to the necessity of maintaining that courts must close their eyes on the Constitution, and see only the law.

This doctrine would subvert the very foundation of all written Constitutions. It would declare that an act which, according to the principles and theory of our government, is entirely void, is yet, in practice, completely obligatory. It would declare that, if the Legislature shall do what is expressly forbidden, such act, notwithstanding the express prohibition, is in reality effectual. It would be giving to the Legislature a practical and real omnipotence with the same breath which professes to restrict their powers within narrow limits. It is prescribing limits, and declaring that those limits may be passed at pleasure.

That it thus reduces to nothing what we have deemed the greatest improvement on political institutions—a written Constitution, would of itself be sufficient, in America where written Constitutions have been viewed with so much reverence, for rejecting the construction. But the peculiar expressions of the Constitution of the United States furnish additional arguments in favor of its rejection.

The judicial power of the United States is extended to all cases arising under the Constitution.

Could it be the intention of those who gave this power to say that, in using it, the Constitution should not be looked into? That a case arising under the Constitution should be decided without examining the instrument under which it arises? This is too extravagant to be maintained.

In some cases then, the Constitution must be looked into by the judges. And if they can open it at all, what part of it are they forbidden to read or to obey?

There are many other parts of the Constitution which serve to illustrate this subject.

It is declared that "no tax or duty shall be laid on articles exported from any State." Suppose a duty on the export of cotton, of tobacco, or of flour, and a suit instituted to recover it. Ought judgment to be rendered in such a case? ought the judges to close their eyes on the Constitution, and only see the law?

The Constitution declares that "no bill of attainder or *ex post facto* law shall be passed."

If, however, such a bill should be passed and a person should be prosecuted under it, must the Court condemn to death those victims whom the Constitution endeavours to preserve?

"No person," says the Constitution, "shall be convicted of treason unless on the testimony of two witnesses to the same overt act, or on confession in open court."

Here, the language of the Constitution is addressed especially to the Courts. It prescribes, directly for them, a rule of evidence not to be departed from. If the Legislature should change that rule, and declare one witness, or a confession out of court, sufficient for conviction, must the constitutional principle yield to the legislative act?

From these and many other selections which might be made, it is apparent that the framers of the Constitution contemplated that instrument as a rule for the government of courts, as well as of the Legislature.

Why otherwise does it direct the judges to take an oath to support it? This oath certainly applies in an especial manner to their conduct in their official character. How immoral to impose it on them if they were to be used as the instruments, and the knowing instruments, for violating what they swear to support!

The oath of office, too, imposed by the Legislature, is completely demonstrative of the legislative opinion on this subject. It is in these words:

> I do solemnly swear that I will administer justice without respect to persons, and do equal right to the poor and to the rich; and that I will faithfully and impartially discharge all the duties incumbent on me as according to the best of

my abilities and understanding, agreeably to the Constitution and laws of the United States.

Why does a judge swear to discharge his duties agreeably to the Constitution of the United States if that Constitution forms no rule for his government? if it is closed upon him and cannot be inspected by him?

If such be the real state of things, this is worse than solemn mockery. To prescribe or to take this oath becomes equally a crime.

It is also not entirely unworthy of observation that, in declaring what shall be the supreme law of the land, the Constitution itself is first mentioned, and not the laws of the United States generally, but those only which shall be made in pursuance of the Constitution, have that rank.

Thus, the particular phraseology of the Constitution of the United States confirms and strengthens the principle, supposed to be essential to all written Constitutions, that a law repugnant to the Constitution is void, and that courts, as well as other departments, are bound by that instrument.

....

Behavioral Theory of Organizations

The behavioral theory of organizations seeks to bridge the gap between science and politics by reexamining the motivation of groups and individuals in the political decision-making process. As a student and now research professor, one of the most fascinating aspects of bounded rationality and political change is the premise that a science relying on behavioral

choice theory will be drawn toward the study of how individuals, groups, and systems process information and solve problems. An analysis of any civic problem and the requisite advocacy needed for change must include the challenges of human thinking and behavior outlined in this excerpt.

....

from

Bounded Rationality and Political Science: Lessons from Public Administration and Public Policy

Journal of Public Administration Research and Theory 13.4 (2003): 399–407.[2]

Bryan Jones

Principle of Trade-Offs

It became evident very early in the study of human choice that people have a difficult time trading off one goal against another when making a choice (Slovak 1990; Tetlock 2000). The classical economic model depicts trade-offs as smooth indifference curves, and modem rational choice theory offers little new in the theoretical study of trade-offs. The first behavioral tool for understanding trade-offs was Simon's notion of satisficing. His idea that a person within an organization chooses alternatives that are "good enough" led critics to claim that the notion was just a poverty-stricken version of maximization. Recently, for example, Lupia, McCubbins, and Popkin claimed that bounded rationality was consistent with maximizing behavior. They cited with approval Jensen and Meckling, who wrote that the use of the term *satisficing* "undoubtedly contributed to this confusion because it suggests rejection of maximizing behavior rather than maximization subject to costs of information and decision making" (2000, 9).

If one adds information and decision-making cost constraints to choice, this will not cause bounded rationality to dissolve into maximizing behavior. The reason is that satisficing describes the cognitive

---

[2]   Bryan Jones, "Bounded Rationality and Political Science: Lessons from Public Administration and Public Policy," *Journal of Public Administration Research and Theory,* vol. 13, no. 4, pp. 399–407. Copyright © 2003 by Oxford University Press. Reprinted with permission.

difficulties people have with trade-offs. As a consequence, satisficing has little to do with some sort of second-rate maximization approach. Because of limited attention spans, people generally work on goals sequentially. As a consequence, trade-offs among goals are very difficult. The response, argued Simon, was for people to set aspiration levels for the goals they wish to achieve. If a choice was good enough (that is, if it exceeded aspiration levels) for all goals, then it was chosen.

Other models of choice among multiple goals have been developed, including the lexicographic strategy (choose the strategy that maximizes gain on the most salient goal and ignore the rest) and elimination by aspects (use a lexicographic strategy unless there is a tie among alternatives; then and only then use a second goal to break the tie). People have considerable difficulty in trading off benefits against losses, which is something that standard utility maximization theory recognizes as straightforward (Kahneman and Tversky 1979).

The Behavioral Theory of Choice

While great strides have been made in recent years by psychologists and behavioral economists who study choices in controlled laboratory arrangements, only serious field study can indicate how choices are made in the structured yet dynamic environments of real-world situations. Bounded rationality and the behavioral theory of choice came from organization theory; indeed, March (1994) once noted that breakthroughs in the study of human cognition were likely to come from a study of organizations. Psychological and behavioral economics have focused almost exclusively on experimental studies and have suffered accordingly. Findings of systematic violations of principles of behavior based on expected utility calculation are dramatic and widespread (Camerer 1998; Camerer and Thaler 1995; Thaler 1991, 1992), yet this says little about choice in the field where behavior can be adaptive and responsive to multiple feedback streams (Laitin 1999).

Behavioral economists have called their writings "the anomalies literature" (Thaler 1988, 1992) because of their single-minded focus on experimental design and their rejection of various tenets of expected utility. Several political scientists have criticized experimental psychology and behavioral economics literature for their seeming ad hoc nature—they build findings experimental effect by experimental effect. They noted correctly that experimentation was a very soft foundation from which to study institutions and macropolitics. From another perspective, David Laitin (1999) properly noted that in everyday actions people were adaptive and avoided many of the traps set for them in experiments. But rather than explore the ramifications of this observation empirically, he jumped to the wholly unwarranted conclusion that people must be comprehensively rational.

There is no support for these and related lines of argument because the behavioral model of choice has been available since the late 1950s. It avoids the anomalies problem, is parsimonious, and, as I shall argue, yields more accurate predictions on aggregates than comprehensive rationality does.

Bounded rationality points to the limits of rational adaptation; behavioral choice theory provides a body of literature that shows how human choice works. As I noted above, bounded rationality and the associated behavioral theory of choice is open ended; we do not know everything about human choice, but we learn more every year. We do know enough to specify the outlines of what aspects of human cognition must be incorporated to formulate a general theory of human choice. I would cite the following:

1. *Long-term memory.* People learn by encoding direct or secondary experience into rules that specify actions to be taken in response to categories of stimuli.

2. *Short-term memory.* Human cognitive capacities include a "front end" that extracts features from the world around them, categorizes them as relevant or irrelevant (in the former case, they become stimuli), and prioritizes them.

3. *Emotions.* In an initial encounter with a choice situation, the major mechanism for weighting the relevance of stimuli is emotion.

4. *Central versus peripheral processing.* When attention and emotion are aroused, information processing shifts toward problem analysis and search. When they are not aroused, the decision maker relies on prepackaged solutions.

5. *The preparation-search trade-off.* If the front-end system indicates a need for action, people can take two paths: They can draw upon previously prepared and stored rules specifying

how to respond to the category that a stimulus has been placed in, or they can search for new responses.

6. *Identification.* People identify emotionally with the previously prepared solutions they have encoded in memory. They become attached emotionally to their current repertoire of encoded solutions, even as the problems they face evolve.

Clearly these six aspects of human cognition do not tell the whole story. For example, in many cases in which attention and emotion are aroused, people may insist on following old rules. But these aspects cover much ground and lay the basis for a general behavioral theory of choice in organizations and institutions.

While organizations clearly free people by extending their capacities to achieve goals, they can also fall prey to aspects of human cognitive architecture in predictable ways. Major aspects of the behavioral theory of organization mirror major facets of the behavioral theory of human choice.

1. *Organizational memory.* Organizations encode experiences into rules, routines, and standard operating procedures that specify actions to be taken in response to categories of stimuli.

2. *Agenda setting.* Organizational capacities include a "front end" that extracts features from the world, categorizes them as relevant or irrelevant (in the former case, they become stimuli), and prioritizes them. Agenda setting in organizations is similar to the short-term memory's affect on human cognition.

3. *Parallel processing.* Organizations expand human capacities by providing people with the ability to process information in a parallel fashion. By decentralizing and delegating, organizations can process multiple streams of input simultaneously (Simon 1983; Jones 1994). This organizational strategy presupposes considerable "peripheral processing" that relies on preprogrammed solutions.

4. *Serial processing.* A search for new solutions is activated only when previously prepared solutions encoded in

organizational routines are judged inadequate. Then organizations move from peripheral to central processing (or from parallel processing to serial processing).

5. *Emotional contagion*. In policy making, emotional commitment and contagion are crucial elements in mobilizing for major initiatives. Moving from parallel to serial processing is invariably accompanied by participants' emotional arousal (Jones 1994).

6. *Identification*. People identify emotionally as well as cognitively with the organizations they participate in. This is a great resource for leaders. Having pride in performing a job can push people to actions that would be unthinkable in a calm cost-benefit analysis. But it can also make it difficult for leaders to shift strategies when they find it necessary to do so.

The relationships between organizational decision making and individual decision making are causal, not metaphorical (Jones 2001). One cannot really understand how organizations operate without a strong sense of how individuals process information and make decisions. As a consequence, a firm scientific foundation for policy studies must be rooted in a behavioral approach to organizations (see Green and Thompson 2001).

Prediction in Science: Inference from Individual Behavior to Collective Choice

Few social scientists today would disagree with Simon's premise that a sound organizational theory must rest on a defensible theory of human behavior. Bounded rationality is more open ended in its basics than the rational model. How much should an unrealistic model of the behavioral underpinnings of collective choice that is nevertheless well specified be traded off against a model that is more realistic but less well specified? In making a judgment, we ought to apply scientific standards. Here the primary standard ought to be the extent to which the model in question can be used to understand and predict collective choices.

Thick and Thin Rationality
Original formulations of rationality assumed self-interest, which can predict individual behaviors and collective choices. Often, however,

people do not seem to act out of self-interest. Experimental studies have been unequivocal on the issue: In laboratory settings, many people do not act out of strictly selfish motives. Frolich and Oppenheimer found that "a substantial set of individuals consider the welfare of others as a value in itself" (2000, 106; for a review of this rich topic, see chapter 5 of Jones 2001).

As a consequence, a "thin" version of rationality was proposed to replace the incorrect "thick" version. Thin rationality ignores the postulate of goals and focuses only on the process—it assumes maximizing behavior regardless of what a person's goals are. Unfortunately this theory leads nowhere because it generates no specific predictions about behavior (Simon 1985). If people have goals that reflect both self-interest and the welfare of others, and formal theorists have no ways of specifying the trade-offs, then no predictions can be made. In the famous "divide the dollar" experiments, in which subjects were asked to divide a prize between themselves and others, specific predictions were made using the postulate of thick rationality, but any division was consistent with the postulate of thin rationality.

To make predictions we would need to study the formation of the reasons people use for the decisions they make. This is equivalent to exploring preference formation and doing it inductively because there are no a priori reasons (on the part of the investigator) for assuming any particular set of reasons (on the part of the subject). If we are going to go this far, why not treat the mechanisms of choices as subject to empirical study, rather than assuming maximization given the unspecified set of reasons used by the decision maker?

Process or Outcome Predictions?

Predictions can be made based on processes or on outcomes. It has traditionally been conceded by proponents of rational choice that the approach was insufficient to predict processes but that it mattered little. The instrumental positivist position, first articulated by Milton Friedman, insisted that predictions are made not on processes but on outcomes (Friedman 1996). Outcome predictions are satisfactory when decision makers act as if they are rational maximizers. Bounded rationality insists that these processes matter and that successful science must properly link the process of individual decision making to organizational processes responsible for collective choices. If that is done successfully, then the outcome predictions will take care of themselves.

The first set of serious predictions using bounded rationality to study public policy came from the budget studies of Wildavsky (1964) and his colleagues and Fenno (1966).[3] Explicitly relying on bounded rationality, these scholars reasoned that budgets ought to be incremental, supported by organizational decision-rules that would stabilize the environment for participants. They examined the process of budgeting directly, and they examined the pattern of budgetary outcomes.

The problem is that public budgets are not incremental, at least when viewed from a long-enough time span or in a broad-enough sample (True 2000; Jones, Baumgartner, and True 1996). The processes underlying incremental budgeting may have been misspecified (Padgett 1980, 1981). Indeed, new budgetary studies, based on outcome predictions but reliant on a proper appreciation of organizational processes, pointed to a glaring omission in earlier budget studies. Focused as they were on organizational procedures that stabilize and make predictable a potentially chaotic environment, earlier studies missed how organizations cope with unexpected change.

There are times when organizations must adjust their standard operating procedures to address signals from the environment that simply cannot be placed within preexisting categories. Padgett's (1980, 1981) examination of federal budget routines found that sequential search for acceptable alternatives under conditions of changing political constraints would yield punctuated change.[4] Carpenter (1996) showed that federal agencies often ignore the budgetary signals sent by Congress unless those signals are sent repeatedly. The first attempt to cope with a radically changing environment seems to be to use the preexisting set of rules; only when it becomes clear that the signals cannot be ignored will an agency respond (at the cost of considerable disruption to internal procedures).

Similarly, the FDA's shift from a priority of protecting public health to one of promoting as well as protecting health had characteristics of a punctuated equilibrium (Ceccoli 2003). In any case, a smooth

---

3   Wildavsky 1964 relied in part on data from Fenno, later published in 1966. In his introduction (1966, xxiv), Fenno described all of the major organizational changes that were eliminated from his data set. Incorporating these changes implies a far different budgeting process.

4   Padgett's work on budgeting was based in organizational processes and developed a decisional mechanism that implied not solely incremental budgetary outputs. These insights did not result in further understanding of the bounded rationality base of budgeting for a decade and a half, testimony to the lags in adaptation in the research enterprise.

response to the problem was not possible because old decision-rules had to be abandoned and replaced by new ones. This leads to episodic, disjointed behavior.

While the early budget studies had much of the budgeting process right, they didn't properly appreciate the role of shifting attention. The allocation of attention is a critical component of agenda-setting studies (Cohen, March, and Olsen 1972; Kingdon 1996; Baumgartner and Jones 1993). Attention shifts in policy making imply changes in standard operating procedures, which in turn predict major punctuations in policy outcomes. So policy outcomes should be characterized by periods of stability or incremental adjustment that are punctuated by periods of rapid change. Further, both stability and change should be more pronounced than the information coming in to the organization (or, more generally, the policy subsystem); that is, whatever the information flow, a model of organizational processes based in bounded rationality predicts a more episodic process in outcomes. Both individuals and organizations are disproportionate information processors when they ignore many signals in the environment until they must overreact (Jones 2001).

Attention-Driven Choice in Political Science and Public Administration

A political science relying on behavioral choice theory will invariably be drawn toward the study of information processing and problem solving. It will be somewhat less focused on questions of equilibrium and control, because these subjects have been attended to far out of proportion to their explanatory power. The nature of behavioral assumptions influences the choice of topics for study.

To illustrate my point, I turn to the study of public administration. Public administration was once at the very vital core of political science—it is, after all, where the great post war debates about rationality and democratic control of policy making were first vigorously pursued. The quality of recent scholarship on public administration may indicate a reemergence of the field.

But there is a vast difference. The early students of public administration were concerned with how organizations and democracy were intermeshed or whether a pluralism of interests generated by Roosevelt's "alphabet soup" of regulatory agencies could fit with a single overhead control model of democracy. On the contrary, much recent high-quality scholarship has collapsed into the single issue of control—and control solely through formal incentives (primarily punishment). The rich insights of behavioral choice have devolved into a discredited Skinnerian psychology, where the incentive controls the behavior.[5]

This is a clear instance of attention-driven choice. The fascination with principal-agent models and the force-fitting of them into complex legislative, executive, and bureaucratic interactions has occupied such a disproportionate amount of attention that it has come close to excluding the traditional broad-gauged questions that dominated the postwar field.

Principal-Agency

The modem literature on public administration indicates that the primary problem—perhaps the only problem—for the study of bureaucracy is control. Bureaucrats seem to spend their lives avoiding doing what superiors want them to do. The primary theoretical vehicle for this extensive line of research is the principal-agent model. This model is based on asymmetric information—an agent has more information than a principal in his or her area of expertise and will invariably use that information to cheat the principal unless formal incentives are in place to make sure that this does not happen.

The model was developed for such situations as when a company hired an accountant, but it has been adapted enthusiastically to the study of legislative-bureau relationships. Strangely enough, the model seems to have been more popular in the United States, where the separation of powers makes the model problematic, than in parliamentary systems, where it may well be more relevant. There are two major problems with this model: (1) it is based on an antiquated model of human behavior (basically Skinnerian psychology), and (2) its incredible popularity has led to a vast overinvestment of scholarly resources in the study of control to the exclusion of other worthy topics.

The adoption of an antiquated (or incorrect) model of human behavior has led to truly strange circumstances in the field. Models based on principal-agency have big problems in confirmation (see Brehm and Gates 1997; Balia 1998; Carpenter 1996; Balia and Wright 2001). Most interesting is Brehm and Gates's commentary that "the primary contribution is … our finding of the overwhelming

---

[5]   It is ironic that Skinner's study of pigeons and mice and the comprehensive rationality of economics both lead to the same impoverished model of human choice: Only formal incentives matter.

importance of attributes of the organizational culture in determining subordinates' levels of compliance" (1993, 578). This is surprising (as Brehm and Gates are well aware) only if one begins with a bad model. Organizational culture is no longer some sort of residual variable but a powerful component of properly formulated analyses (Miller 1992).

What does one do if one finds a general lack of confirmation of the purest principal-agent models in government agencies? The "as if" school of thought requires disconfirmation. What do we disconfirm? That control in organizations is not relevant? That the principal-agent distinction is not valid? That asymmetric information does not occur in bureaucracies? All of these would be silly but are required by followers of Milton Friedman. What is not valid is the outmoded model of human behavior that the principal-agent model is based on. Get rid of the antiquated assumption, and a better perspective on the role of control in bureaucracies emerges.

Administrative Procedures

Perhaps in no other area of public administration has more effort been directed in an inefficient fashion than in the "deck stacking" thesis of McCubbins, Noll, and Weingast (1987). This theory even comes with its own pet name: "McNollgast." As is usual in principal-agent-based theorizing, Congress is obsessed with the control of bureaucrats and sets up administrative procedures to empower interests comprising the majority coalition. Yet key components of the Administrative Procedures Act of 1946 require "notice and comment" before the issuance of regulations.

On the face of it, this looks more like issuing rules to stabilize an uncertain environment, maybe even solving the problem of every debate about regulations being appealed to Congress.[6] Organizational routines focus attention toward certain aspects of the environment and exclude others, and these routines also regularize the responses to environmental stimuli. It has always been assumed that such rules may carry a bias, but the empirical documentation of such bias (outside of the questionable bias of allowing the interested the opportunity to participate in a democracy) has been difficult.[7] In any case, good

---

6   I thank Gary Miller for pointing this out.

7   This was exactly the question that motivated the urban service distribution literature of the 1970s and 1980s. The consensus drawn from numerous empirical studies was that services were delivered according to decision-rules that favored those willing to make routine demands on government; see Jones 1980, Linberry 1977, Mladenka 1978.

science would have required the explicit exclusion on theoretical or empirical grounds before leaping to an overhead control model.

If McNollgast was poor science, at least it was a compelling and innovative hypothesis. One wonders why, given the extraordinary attention this piece received, no scholar pointed out its inconsistencies or the inconsistencies of other hypotheses from behavioral organization theory.

Principal-Agency, Deck Stacking, and Sound Science

The focus on principal-agency at the expense of more scientifically based perspectives is a selection device. It leads directly to an overemphasis on control as well as other important mistakes. These include

1. *Isolating out one motive from a panoply of those that drive congressional behavior.* If members of Congress are focused fundamentally on reelection, then the right question is how they balance (or trade off) the various means that could lead to that goal. One way could be controlling bureaucratic behavior. The behavioral model of choice would insist that this balancing is accomplished via attentional mechanisms. How various means to goals get activated is a critical component of choice, but this is completely ignored in the congressional literature.

2. *Ignoring the fundamental role of uncertainty.* Behavioral choice implies that uncertainty in decision making is fundamental. In principal-agent relations, uncertainty is fundamental to both parties. Complaining that the principal-agent model fails to specify how agencies make decisions, George Krause (2003, 186) notes that uncertainty is treated similarly as an assumption or an afterthought. His work suggests that it is fundamental to the process. Most problems that matter in agency decision making are not the well-structured ones of formalistic analysis but ill-structured ones that infuse uncertainty throughout the decision-making process.

3. *Dismissing aspects of "organizational culture," in particular the well-documented phenomenon of "identification with the means,"* Start with a principal-agent formulation based on a discredited microfoundation, and invariably the result is a call to study

the internal dynamics of agencies. Start with a more robust microfoundation of behavior, and a more robust organizational analysis emerges.

Attention-Driven Choice and Identification with the Means in Public Agencies

The basis for the behavioral model of choice is the processing of information. Information is not predefined or prepackaged; rather it is often vague, ambiguous, and, most importantly, generated from multiple sources. Unlike the equilibrium-based analyses of principal-agency, it is dynamic. The receiver of the information is as important as the sender (Jones 2001).

An information-processing perspective leads to a richer and more scientifically sound approach to public policy and public administration than the cramped and formalistic control perspective currently in vogue in the field. In modern complex environments, neither individuals nor organizations respond simply to stimuli. They must attend, prioritize, and select an appropriate response. As a consequence, there is no clear, one-to-one mapping between potential stimuli or events and actions.

A major key to understanding information processing in people and organizations is the allocation of attention. A few examples illustrate how an information-processing approach compares with the current principal-agent fascination.

In the Inspector General's Office of the Social Security Administration, investigators in field offices study complaints of illegalities and choose whether to proceed against the alleged perpetrators. The central office is crystal clear about how to prioritize crimes: Move against those that will return the most money to the U.S. Treasury. Individual investigators may decide what cases are likely to bring the largest return, but they have no discretion to substitute their priorities for those of the central office. Of course control cannot be insured except through some type of records or on-site monitoring. So it looks like a classic principal-agent delegation-type problem.

However, it is not as it seems. If field offices followed the central dictate to the letter, organizational chaos would be the most likely result. In effect, the central office does not want the announced priority system to be followed. When a "hot" case, one with some degree of media interest, emerges, the old priorities are not valid. If a criminal cheats a handful of widows of their Social Security checks, causing destitution on a small scale, the agency cannot defend itself through its control mechanisms. Able agents quickly realize that the argument about preventing potentially hot cases from exploding could act as a defense against charges that they were violating central office policy. If central control were pursued to the exclusion of anticipatory problem solving, punishing those showing initiative, soon the agency would devolve into a pathological one, incapable of responding to changing circumstances. In effect, most managers do not really want control. They want adaptive information processing.[8]

In his study of municipal budgeting, John Crecine (1969) noted that city agencies developed attention rules, which indicated what aspects of the environment ought to be monitored for indicators of change that could need addressing. These rules did not tell the agency what to do, only what to attend to. Similarly Jones (1985) found in a study of Chicago building-code enforcement that informal norms generally supplanted the complexities of the code, but that supervisors occasionally sent out signals to field inspectors that all violations were to be recorded in potentially hot cases. These cases, usually when there was party, neighborhood group, or media interest, simply generated better code enforcement than the bulk of cases. Differential code enforcement resulted as a consequence of these attention rules.

Research by Armstrong, Carpenter, and Hojnacki (2003) indicates that media attention to disease is not simply related to mortality and morbidity. This attention seems to mediate output indicators, such as investment in cures and related science. The designation of a hot disease has characteristics of a disjointed response to objective disease characteristics.

Attention is different from any other resource type variable because one cannot allocate it proportionally to one's priorities at any one time. Attention is selective; select one aspect of an environment for study and inattention must be paid to the rest of the environment. Attention is partially under the control of a decision maker, but cognitively that decision maker possesses no comprehensive system for monitoring when enough attention has been devoted to a topic. As a consequence, shifts in attentiveness are in large part due to emotional

---

8   This example is based on an undergraduate student paper. Interestingly, the SSA refused to allow the development of this example into an extended paper for publication.

arousal. Attention shifts are governed by emotion, so they are un-avoidably disrupted. Past decisions are a residue of past allocations of attention because, in many cases, the devotion of other resources follows attention. Decisions may or may not be consistent—great inconsistencies in choices are a result of the level of attention.

Identification with the Means

Bound up with any change in decision-rules is identification with the means rather than ends, a key factor in policy choice and implemen-tation (and first isolated as a key aspect of organizational behavior by Simon in *Administrative Behavior*). People in organizations identify emo-tionally and cognitively with operating procedures, and this nonrational process compounds the disjointed adjustment behavior in bureaus.

In one of the last pieces Simon published, he and Ronald Fernandes (1999) applied the process-tracing methodology initially developed by Newell and Simon (1972) in their problem-solving experiments to the complex and ill-structured problems characteristic of policy issues. Fernandes and Simon showed that the initial problem-solving experiments studied well-specified problems, but the methods them-selves are adaptable to less-structured situations. They wondered if the professional identifications led to different problem-solving strategies. One intriguing finding was the dominance of a Know → Recommend strategy among many participants, which hindered their use of information in problem solving.

....

Federalist Paper No. 47

The doctrine of separation of powers centers on the tendency for power to be consolidated under one despot. It is difficult to imagine the potentiality for a takeover of all government agencies by a single charismatic individual. What is more likely and much easier to imagine is a process by which many antidemocratic individuals who lack a political connection form a new group to advocate for their preferences and interests over those of the whole. There are many readings from the formation of this constitutional government that express this fear, but Federalist Paper No. 47 provides a historical and contemporary account of the state of mind of the framers as they moved through the Constitution-making process.

....

from

The New York Packet

The Particular Structure of the New Government and the Distribution of Power Among Its Different Parts[9] Friday, February 1, 1788.

James Madison

To the People of the State of New York:

Having reviewed the general form of the proposed government and the general mass of power allotted to it, I proceed to examine the particular structure of this government, and the distribution of this mass of power among its constituent parts. One of the principal objections inculcated by the more respectable adversaries to the Constitution, is its supposed violation of the political maxim, that the legislative, executive, and judiciary departments ought to be separate and distinct.

In the structure of the federal government, no regard, it is said, seems to have been paid to this essential precaution in favor of liberty. The several departments of power are distributed and blended in such a manner as at once to destroy all symmetry and beauty of form, and to expose some of the essential parts of the edifice to the danger of being crushed by the disproportionate weight of other parts. No political truth is certainly of greater intrinsic value, or is stamped with the authority of more enlightened patrons of liberty, than that on which the objection is founded.

The accumulation of all powers, legislative, executive, and judiciary, in the same hands, whether of one, a few, or many, and whether hereditary, self-appointed, or elective, may justly be pronounced the very definition of tyranny. Were the federal Constitution, therefore, really chargeable with the accumulation of power, or with a mixture

---

9   James Madison, "The Federalist Papers: No. 47," *The New York Packet,* Friday, February 1, 1788. Copyright in the Public Domain.

of powers, having a dangerous tendency to such an accumulation, no further arguments would be necessary to inspire a universal reprobation of the system. I persuade myself, however, that it will be made apparent to every one, that the charge cannot be supported, and that the maxim on which it relies has been totally misconceived and misapplied. In order to form correct ideas on this important subject, it will be proper to investigate the sense in which the preservation of liberty requires that the three great departments of power should be separate and distinct. The oracle who is always consulted and cited on this subject is the celebrated Montesquieu. If he be not the author of this invaluable precept in the science of politics, he has the merit at least of displaying and recommending it most effectually to the attention of mankind. Let us endeavor, in the first place, to ascertain his meaning on this point. The British Constitution was to Montesquieu what Homer has been to the didactic writers on epic poetry. As the latter have considered the work of the immortal bard as the perfect model from which the principles and rules of the epic art were to be drawn, and by which all similar works were to be judged, so this great political critic appears to have viewed the Constitution of England as the standard, or to use his own expression, as the mirror of political liberty; and to have delivered, in the form of elementary truths, the several characteristic principles of that particular system. That we may be sure, then, not to mistake his meaning in this case, let us recur to the source from which the maxim was drawn.

On the slightest view of the British Constitution, we must perceive that the legislative, executive, and judiciary departments are by no means totally separate and distinct from each other. The executive magistrate forms an integral part of the legislative authority. He alone has the prerogative of making treaties with foreign sovereigns, which, when made, have, under certain limitations, the force of legislative acts. All the members of the judiciary department are appointed by him, can be removed by him on the address of the two Houses of Parliament, and form, when he pleases to consult them, one of his constitutional councils. One branch of the legislative department forms also a great constitutional council to the executive chief, as, on another hand, it is the sole depositary of judicial power in cases of impeachment, and is invested with the supreme appellate jurisdiction in all other cases. The judges, again, are so far connected with the legislative department as often to attend and participate in its deliberations, though not admitted to a legislative vote. From these facts, by which Montesquieu was guided, it may clearly be inferred that, in saying "There can be no liberty where the legislative and executive powers are united in the same person, or body of magistrates," or, "if the power of judging be not separated from the legislative and executive powers," he did not mean that these departments ought to have no PARTIAL AGENCY in, or no CONTROL over, the acts of each other. His meaning, as his own words import, and still more conclusively as illustrated by the example in his eye, can amount to no more than this, that where the WHOLE power of one department is exercised by the same hands which possess the WHOLE power of another department, the fundamental principles of a free constitution are subverted. This would have been the case in the constitution examined by him, if the king, who is the sole executive magistrate, had possessed also the complete legislative power, or the supreme administration of justice; or if the entire legislative body had possessed the supreme judiciary, or the supreme executive authority.

This, however, is not among the vices of that constitution. The magistrate in whom the whole executive power resides cannot of himself make a law, though he can put a negative on every law; nor administer justice in person, though he has the appointment of those who do administer it. The judges can exercise no executive prerogative, though they are shoots from the executive stock; nor any legislative function, though they may be advised with by the legislative councils. The entire legislature can perform no judiciary act, though by the joint act of two of its branches the judges may be removed from their offices, and though one of its branches is possessed of the judicial power in the last resort. The entire legislature, again, can exercise no executive prerogative, though one of its branches constitutes the supreme executive magistracy, and another, on the impeachment of a third, can try and condemn all the subordinate officers in the executive department. The reasons on which Montesquieu grounds his maxim are a further demonstration of his meaning. "When the legislative and executive powers are united in the same person or body," says he, "there can be no liberty, because apprehensions may arise lest THE SAME monarch or senate should ENACT tyrannical laws to EXECUTE them in a tyrannical manner." Again: "Were the power of judging joined with the legislative, the life and liberty of the subject would be exposed to arbitrary control, for THE JUDGE would then be THE LEGISLATOR. Were it joined to the executive power, THE JUDGE might behave with all the violence of

AN OPPRESSOR." Some of these reasons are more fully explained in other passages; but briefly stated as they are here, they sufficiently establish the meaning which we have put on this celebrated maxim of this celebrated author.

If we look into the constitutions of the several States, we find that, notwithstanding the emphatical and, in some instances, the unqualified terms in which this axiom has been laid down, there is not a single instance in which the several departments of power have been kept absolutely separate and distinct. New Hampshire, whose constitution was the last formed, seems to have been fully aware of the impossibility and inexpediency of avoiding any mixture whatever of these departments, and has qualified the doctrine by declaring "that the legislative, executive, and judiciary powers ought to be kept as separate from, and independent of, each other AS THE NATURE OF A FREE GOVERNMENT WILL ADMIT; OR AS IS CONSISTENT WITH THAT CHAIN OF CONNECTION THAT BINDS THE WHOLE FABRIC OF THE CONSTITUTION IN ONE INDISSOLUBLE BOND OF UNITY AND AMITY." Her constitution accordingly mixes these departments in several respects. The Senate, which is a branch of the legislative department, is also a judicial tribunal for the trial of impeachments. The President, who is the head of the executive department, is the presiding member also of the Senate; and, besides an equal vote in all cases, has a casting vote in case of a tie. The executive head is himself eventually elective every year by the legislative department, and his council is every year chosen by and from the members of the same department. Several of the officers of state are also appointed by the legislature. And the members of the judiciary department are appointed by the executive department. The constitution of Massachusetts has observed a sufficient though less pointed caution, in expressing this fundamental article of liberty. It declares "that the legislative department shall never exercise the executive and judicial powers, or either of them; the executive shall never exercise the legislative and judicial powers, or either of them; the judicial shall never exercise the legislative and executive powers, or either of them." This declaration corresponds precisely with the doctrine of Montesquieu, as it has been explained, and is not in a single point violated by the plan of the convention. It goes no farther than to prohibit any one of the entire departments from exercising the powers of another department. In the very Constitution to which it is prefixed, a partial mixture of powers has been admitted.

The executive magistrate has a qualified negative on the legislative body, and the Senate, which is a part of the legislature, is a court of impeachment for members both of the executive and judiciary departments. The members of the judiciary department, again, are appointable by the executive department, and removable by the same authority on the address of the two legislative branches. Lastly, a number of the officers of government are annually appointed by the legislative department.

As the appointment to offices, particularly executive offices, is in its nature an executive function, the compilers of the Constitution have, in this last point at least, violated the rule established by themselves. I pass over the constitutions of Rhode Island and Connecticut, because they were formed prior to the Revolution, and even before the principle under examination had become an object of political attention. The constitution of New York contains no declaration on this subject; but appears very clearly to have been framed with an eye to the danger of improperly blending the different departments. It gives, nevertheless, to the executive magistrate, a partial control over the legislative department; and, what is more, gives a like control to the judiciary department; and even blends the executive and judiciary departments in the exercise of this control. In its council of appointment members of the legislative are associated with the executive authority, in the appointment of officers, both executive and judiciary. And its court for the trial of impeachments and correction of errors is to consist of one branch of the legislature and the principal members of the judiciary department.

The constitution of New Jersey has blended the different powers of government more than any of the preceding. The governor, who is the executive magistrate, is appointed by the legislature; is chancellor and ordinary, or surrogate of the State; is a member of the Supreme Court of Appeals, and president, with a casting vote, of one of the legislative branches. The same legislative branch acts again as executive council of the governor, and with him constitutes the Court of Appeals. The members of the judiciary department are appointed by the legislative department and removable by one branch of it, on the impeachment of the other. According to the constitution of Pennsylvania, the president, who is the head of the executive department, is annually elected by a vote in which the legislative department predominates. In conjunction with an executive council, he appoints the members of the judiciary department, and forms a court of impeachment for trial of all officers, judiciary as well as executive. The judges of the Supreme Court and justices of the peace seem also to be removable by the legislature; and the executive power of pardoning in certain cases, to be referred to the same department. The members of the executive council are made EX-OFFICIO justices of peace throughout the State. In Delaware, the chief executive magistrate is annually elected by the legislative department. The speakers of the two legislative branches are vice-presidents in the executive department. The executive chief, with six others, appointed, three by each of the legislative branches constitutes the Supreme Court of Appeals; he is joined with the legislative department in the appointment of the other judges. Throughout the States, it appears that the members of the legislature may at the same time be justices of the peace; in this State, the members of one branch of it are EXOFFICIO justices of the peace; as are also the members of the executive council. The principal officers of the executive department are appointed by the legislative; and one branch of the latter forms a court of impeachments. All officers may be removed on address of the legislature.

Maryland has adopted the maxim in the most unqualified terms; declaring that the legislative, executive, and judicial powers of government ought to be forever separate and distinct from each other. Her constitution, notwithstanding, makes the executive magistrate appointable by the legislative department; and the members of the judiciary by the executive department. The language of Virginia is still more pointed on this subject. Her constitution declares, "that the legislative, executive, and judiciary departments shall be separate and distinct; so that neither exercise the powers properly belonging to the other; nor shall any person exercise the powers of more than one of them at the same time, except that the justices of county courts shall be eligible to either House of Assembly." Yet we find not only this express exception, with respect to the members of the inferior courts, but that the chief magistrate, with his executive council, are appointable by the legislature; that two members of the latter are triennially displaced at the pleasure of the legislature; and that all the principal offices, both executive and judiciary, are filled by the same department. The executive prerogative of pardon, also, is in one case vested in the legislative department.

The constitution of North Carolina, which declares "that the legislative, executive, and supreme judicial powers of government ought to be forever separate and distinct from each other," refers, at the same time, to the legislative department, the appointment not only of the executive chief, but all the principal officers within both that and the judiciary department. In South Carolina, the constitution makes the executive magistracy eligible by the legislative department. It gives to the latter, also, the appointment of the members of the judiciary department, including even justices of the peace and sheriffs; and the appointment of officers in the executive department, down to captains in the army and navy of the State. In the constitution of Georgia, where it is declared "that the legislative, executive, and judiciary departments shall be separate and distinct, so that neither exercise the powers properly belonging to the other," we find that the executive department is to be filled by appointments of the legislature; and the executive prerogative of pardon to be finally exercised by the same authority. Even justices of the peace are to be appointed by the legislature.

In citing these cases, in which the legislative, executive, and judiciary departments have not been kept totally separate and distinct, I wish not to be regarded as an advocate for the particular organizations of the several State governments. I am fully aware that among the many excellent principles which they exemplify, they carry strong marks of the haste, and still stronger of the inexperience, under which they were framed. It is but too obvious that in some instances the fundamental principle under consideration has been violated by too great a mixture, and even an actual consolidation, of the different powers; and that in no instance has a competent provision been made for maintaining in practice the separation delineated on paper. What I have wished to evince is, that the charge brought against the proposed Constitution, of violating the sacred maxim of free government, is warranted neither by the real meaning annexed to that maxim by its author, nor by the sense in which it has hitherto been understood in America. This interesting subject will be resumed in the ensuing paper.

PUBLIUS.

....

Confronting Class

Bell Hooks presents an urgent question for critical social science research: How can education better integrate those from the working-class poor and how can educators better understand the point of view of the working class when so many educators in higher education are from privileged backgrounds, often white males with parents who attended college?

....

from

Confronting Class in the Classroom[10]

Class is rarely talked about in the United States; nowhere is there a more intense silence about the reality of class differences than in educational settings. Significantly, class differences are particularly ignored in classrooms. From grade school on, we are all encouraged to cross the threshold of the classroom believing we are entering a democratic space—a free zone where the desire to study and learn makes us all equal. And even if we enter accepting the reality of class differences, most of us still believe knowledge will be meted out in fair and equal proportions. In those rare cases where it is acknowledged that students and professors do not share the same class backgrounds, the underlying assumption is still that we are all equally committed to getting ahead, to moving up the ladder of success to the top. And even though many of us will not make it to the top, the unspoken understanding is that we will land somewhere in the middle, between top and bottom.

Coming from a nonmaterially privileged background, from the working poor, I entered college acutely aware of class. When I received notice of my acceptance at Stanford University, the first question that was raised in my household was how I would pay for it. My parents understood that I had been awarded scholarships, and allowed to take out loans, but they wanted to know where the money would come from for transportation, clothes, books. Given these concerns, I went to Stanford thinking that class was mainly about materiality. It only took me a short while to understand that class was more than just a

---

10   bell hooks, "Confronting Class in the Classroom," *Teaching to Transgress: Education as the Practice of Freedom*, pp. 177–189. Copyright © 1994 by Taylor & Francis Group. Reprinted with permission.

question of money, that it shaped values, attitudes, social relations, and the biases that informed the way knowledge would be given and received. These same realizations about class in the academy are expressed again and again by academics from working-class backgrounds in the collection of essays *Strangers in Paradise* edited by Jake Ryan and Charles Sackrey.

During my college years it was tacitly assumed that we all agreed that class should not be talked about, that there would be no critique of the bourgeois class biases shaping and informing pedagogical process (as well as social etiquette) in the classroom. Although no one ever directly stated the rules that would govern our conduct, it was taught by example and reinforced by a system of rewards. As silence and obedience to authority were most rewarded, students learned that this was the appropriate demeanor in the classroom. Loudness, anger, emotional outbursts, and even something as seemingly innocent as unrestrained laughter were deemed unacceptable, vulgar disruptions of classroom social order. These traits were also associated with being a member of the lower classes. If one was not from a privileged class group, adopting a demeanor similar to that of the group could help one to advance. It is still necessary for students to assimilate bourgeois values in order to be deemed acceptable.

Bourgeois values in the classroom create a barrier, blocking the possibility of confrontation and conflict, warding off dissent. Students are often silenced by means of their acceptance of class values that teach them to maintain order at all costs. When the obsession with maintaining order is coupled with the fear of "losing face," of not being thought well of by one's professor and peers, all possibility of constructive dialogue is undermined. Even though students enter the "democratic" classroom believing they have the right to "free speech," most students are not comfortable exercising this right to "free speech." Most students are not comfortable exercising this right—especially if it means they must give voice to thoughts, ideas, feelings that go against the grain, that are unpopular. This censoring process is only one way bourgeois values overdetermine social behavior in the classroom and undermine the democratic exchange of ideas. Writing about his experience in the section of *Strangers in Paradise* entitled "Outsiders," Karl Anderson confessed:

> Power and hierarchy, and not teaching and learning, dominated the graduate school I found myself in. "Knowledge"

> was one-upmanship, and no one disguised the fact. … The one thing I learned absolutely was the inseparability of free speech and free thought. I, as well as some of my peers, were refused the opportunity to speak and sometimes to ask questions deemed "irrelevant" when the instructors didn't wish to discuss or respond to them.

Students who enter the academy unwilling to accept without question the assumptions and values held by privileged classes tend to be silenced, deemed troublemakers.

Conservative discussions of censorship in contemporary university settings often suggest that the absence of constructive dialogue, enforced silencing, takes place as a by-product of progressive efforts to question canonical knowledge, critique relations of domination, or subvert bourgeois class biases. There is little or no discussion of the way in which the attitudes and values of those from materially privileged classes are imposed upon everyone via biased pedagogical strategies. Reflected in choice of subject matter and the manner in which ideas are shared, these biases need never be overtly stated. In his essay Karl Anderson states that silencing is "the most oppressive aspect of middle-class life." He maintains:

> It thrives upon people keeping their mouths shut, unless they are actually endorsing whatever powers exist. The free marketplace of "ideas" that is so beloved of liberals is as much a fantasy as a free market place in oil or automobiles; a more harmful fantasy, because it breeds even more hypocrisy and cynicism. Just as teachers can control what is said in their class rooms, most also have ultra-sensitive antennae as to what will be rewarded or punished that is said outside them. And these antennae control them.

Silencing enforced by bourgeois values is sanctioned in the classroom by everyone.

Even those professors who embrace the tenets of critical pedagogy (many of whom are white and male) still conduct their classrooms in a manner that only reinforces bourgeois models of decorum. At the same time, the subject matter taught in such classes might reflect professorial awareness of intellectual perspectives that critique domination, that emphasize an understanding of the politics of difference, of race, class, gender, even though classroom dynamics remain conventional, business as usual. When contemporary feminist movement made its initial presence felt in the academy there was both an ongoing critique of conventional classroom dynamics and an attempt to create alternative pedagogical strategies. However, as feminist scholars endeavored to make Women's Studies a discipline administrators and peers would respect, there was a shift in perspective.

Significantly, feminist classrooms were the first spaces in the university where I encountered any attempt to acknowledge class difference. The focus was usually on the way class differences are structured in the larger society, not on our class position. Yet the focus on gender privilege in patriarchal society often meant that there was a recognition of the ways women were economically disenfranchised and therefore more likely to be poor or working class. Often, the feminist classroom was the only place where students (mostly female) from materially disadvantaged circumstances would speak from that class positionality, acknowledging both the impact of class on our social status as well as critiquing the class biases of feminist thought.

When I first entered university settings I felt estranged from this new environment. Like most of my peers and professors, I initially believed those feelings were there because of differences in racial and cultural background. However, as time passed it was more evident that this estrangement was in part a reflection of class difference. At Stanford, I was often asked by peers and professors if I was there on a scholarship. Underlying this question was the implication that receiving financial aid "diminished" one in some way. It was not just this experience that intensified my awareness of class difference, it was the constant evocation of materially privileged class experience (usually that of the middle class) as a universal norm that not only set those of us from working-class backgrounds apart but effectively excluded those who were not privileged from discussions, from social activities. To avoid feelings of estrangement, students from working-class backgrounds could assimilate into the mainstream, change speech patterns, points of reference, drop any habit that might reveal them to be from a nonmaterially privileged background.

Of course I entered college hoping that a university degree would enhance my class mobility. Yet I thought of this solely in economic terms. Early on I did not realize that class was much more than one's economic standing, that it determined values, standpoint, and interests. It was assumed that any student coming from a poor or working-class background would willingly surrender all values and habits of being associated with this background. Those of us from diverse ethnic/racial backgrounds learned that no aspect of our vernacular culture could be voiced in elite settings. This was especially the case with vernacular language or a first language that was not English. To insist on speaking in any manner that did not conform to privileged class ideals and mannerisms placed one always in the position of interloper.

Demands that individuals from class backgrounds deemed undesirable surrender all vestiges of their past create psychic turmoil. We were encouraged, as many students are today, to betray our class origins. Rewarded if we chose to assimilate, estranged if we chose to maintain those aspects of who we were, some were all too often seen as outsiders. Some of us rebelled by clinging to exaggerated manners and behavior clearly marked as outside the accepted bourgeois norm. During my student years, and now as a professor, I see many students from "undesirable" class backgrounds become unable to complete their studies because the contradictions between the behavior necessary to "make it" in the academy and those that allowed them to be comfortable at home, with their families and friends, are just too great.

Often, African Americans are among those students I teach from poor and working-class backgrounds who are most vocal about issues of class. They express frustration, anger, and sadness about the tensions and stress they experience trying to conform to acceptable white, middle-class behaviors in university settings while retaining the ability to "deal" at home. Sharing strategies for coping from my own experience, I encourage students to reject the notion that they must choose between experiences. They must believe they can inhabit comfortably two different worlds, but they must make each space one of comfort. They must creatively invent ways to cross borders. They must believe in their capacity to alter the bourgeois settings they enter. All too often, students from nonmaterially privileged backgrounds assume a position of passivity—they behave as victims, as though they can only be acted upon against their will. Ultimately, they end up feeling they can only reject or accept the norms imposed upon them. This either/or often sets them up for disappointment and failure.

Those of us in the academy from working-class backgrounds are empowered when we recognize our own agency, our capacity to be active participants in the pedagogical process. This process is not simple or easy: it takes courage to embrace a vision of wholeness of being that does not reinforce the capitalist version that suggests that one must always give something up to gain another. In the introduction to the section of their book titled "Class Mobility and Internalized Conflict," Ryan and Sackrey remind readers that "the academic work process is essentially antagonistic to the working class, and academics for the most part live in a different world of culture, different ways that make it, too, antagonistic to working class life." Yet those of us from working-class backgrounds cannot allow class antagonism to prevent us from gaining knowledge, degrees and enjoying the aspects of higher education that are fulfilling. Class antagonism can be constructively used, not made to reinforce the notion that students and professors from working-class backgrounds are "outsiders" and "interlopers," but to subvert and challenge the existing structure.

When I entered my first Women's Studies classes at Stanford, white professors talked about "women" when they were making the experience of materially privileged white women a norm. It was both a matter of personal and intellectual integrity for me to challenge this biased assumption. By challenging, I refused to be complicit in the erasure of black and/or working-class women of all ethnicities. Personally, that meant I was not able just to sit in class, grooving on the good feminist vibes—that was a loss. The gain was that I was honoring the experience of poor and working-class women in my own family, in that very community that had encouraged and supported me in my efforts to be better educated. Even though my intervention was not wholeheartedly welcomed, it created a context for critical thinking, for dialectical exchange.

Any attempt on the part of individual students to critique the bourgeois biases that shape pedagogical process, particularly as they relate to epistemological perspectives (the points from which information is shared) will, in most cases, no doubt, be viewed as negative and disruptive. Given the presumed radical or liberal nature of early feminist classrooms, it was shocking to me to find those settings were also often closed to different ways of thinking. While it was acceptable to critique patriarchy in that context, it was not acceptable to confront issues of class, especially in ways that were not simply about the evocation of guilt. In general, despite their participation in different disciplines and the diversity of class backgrounds, African American scholars and other nonwhite professors have been no more willing to confront issues of class. Even when it became more acceptable to give at least lip service to the recognition of race, gender, and class, most professors and students just did not feel they were able to address class in anything more than a simplistic way. Certainly, the primary area where there was the possibility of meaningful critique and change was in relation to biased scholarship, work that used the experiences and thoughts of materially privileged people as normative.

In recent years, growing awareness of class differences in progressive academic circles has meant that students and professors committed to critical and feminist pedagogy have the opportunity to make spaces in the academy where class can receive attention. Yet there can be no intervention that challenges the status quo if we are not willing to interrogate the way our presentation of self as well as our pedagogical process is often shaped by middle-class norms. My awareness of class has been continually reinforced by my efforts to remain close to loved ones who remain in materially underprivileged class positions. This has helped me to employ pedagogical strategies that create ruptures in the established order, that promote modes of learning which challenge bourgeois hegemony.

One such strategy has been the emphasis on creating in classrooms learning communities where everyone's voice can be heard, their presence recognized and valued. In the section of *Strangers in Paradise* entitled "Balancing Class Locations," Jane Ellen Wilson shares the way an emphasis on personal voice strengthened her.

> Only by coming to terms with my own past, my own background, and seeing that in the context of the world at large, have I begun to find my true voice and to understand that, since it is my own voice, that no pre-cut niche exists for it; that part of the work to be done is making a place, with others, where my and our voices, can stand clear of the background noise and voice our concerns as part of a larger song.

When those of us in the academy who are working class or from working-class backgrounds share our perspectives, we subvert the tendency to focus only on the thoughts, attitudes, and experiences of those who are materially privileged. Feminist and critical pedagogy are two alternative paradigms for teaching which have really emphasized the issue of coming to voice. That focus emerged as central, precisely because it was so evident that race, sex, and class privilege empower some students more than others, granting "authority" to some voices more than others.

A distinction must be made between a shallow emphasis on coming to voice, which wrongly suggests there can be some democratization of voice wherein everyone's words will be given equal time and be seen as equally valuable (often the model applied in feminist classrooms), and the more complex recognition of the uniqueness of each voice and a willingness to create spaces in the classroom where all voices can be heard because all students are free to speak, knowing their presence will be recognized and valued. This does not mean that anything can be said, no matter how irrelevant to classroom subject matter, and receive attention—or that something meaningful takes place if everyone has equal time to voice an opinion. In the classes I teach, I have students write short paragraphs that they read aloud so that we all have a chance to hear unique perspectives and we are all given an opportunity to pause and listen to one another. Just the physical experience of hearing, of listening intently, to each particular voice strengthens our capacity to learn together. Even though a student may not speak again after this moment, that student's presence has been acknowledged.

Hearing each other's voices, individual thoughts, and sometimes associating theses voices with personal experience makes us more acutely aware of each other. That moment of collective participation and dialogue means that students and professor respect—and here I invoke the root meaning of the word, "to look at"—each other, engage in acts of recognition with one another, and do not just talk to the professor. Sharing experiences and confessional narratives in the classroom helps establish communal commitment to learning. These narrative moments usually are the space where the assumption that we share a common class background and perspective is disrupted. While students may be open to the idea that they do not all come from a common class background, they may still expect that the values of materially privileged groups will be the class's norm.

Some students may feel threatened if awareness of class difference leads to changes in the classroom. Today's students all dress alike, wearing clothes from stores such as the Gap and Benetton; this acts to erase the markers of class difference that older generations of students experienced. Young students are more eager to deny the impact of class and class differences in our society. I have found that students from upper- and middle-class backgrounds are disturbed if heated exchange takes place in the classroom. Many of them equate loud talk or interruptions with rude and threatening behavior. Yet those of us from working-class backgrounds may feel that discussion is deeper and richer if it arouses intense responses. In class, students are often disturbed if anyone is interrupted while speaking, even though outside class most of them are not threatened. Few of us are taught to facilitate heated discussions that may include useful interruptions and digressions, but it is often the professor who is most invested in maintaining order in the classroom. Professors cannot empower students to embrace diversities of experience, standpoint, behavior, or style if our training has disempowered us, socialized us to cope effectively only with a single mode of interaction based on middle-class values.

Most progressive professors are more comfortable striving to challenge class biases through the material studied than they are with interrogating how class biases shape conduct in the classroom and transforming their pedagogical process. When I entered my first classroom as a college professor and a feminist, I was deeply afraid of using authority in a way that would perpetuate class elitism and other forms of domination. Fearful that I might abuse power, I falsely pretended that no power difference existed between students and myself. That was a mistake. Yet it was only as I began to interrogate my fear of "power"—the way that fear was related to my own class background where I had so often seen those with class power coerce, abuse, and dominate those without—that I began to understand that power was not itself negative. It depended what one did with it. It was up to me to create ways within my professional power constructively, precisely because I was teaching in institutional structures that affirm it is fine to use power to reinforce and maintain coercive hierarchies.

Fear of losing control in the classroom often leads individual professors to fall into a conventional teaching pattern wherein power is used destructively. It is this fear that leads to collective professorial investment in bourgeois decorum as a means of maintaining a fixed notion of order, of ensuring that the teacher will have absolute authority. Unfortunately, this fear of losing control shapes and informs the professorial pedagogical process to the extent that it acts a barrier preventing any constructive grappling with issues of class.

Sometimes students who want professors to grapple with class differences often simply desire that individuals from less materially privileged backgrounds be given center stage so that an inversion of hierarchical structures takes place, not a disruption. One semester, a number of black female students from working-class backgrounds attended a course I taught on African American women writers. They arrived hoping I would use my professorial power to decenter the voices of privileged white students in nonconstructive ways so that those students would experience what it is like to be an outsider. Some of these black students rigidly resisted attempts to involve the others in an engaged pedagogy where space is created for everyone. Many of the black students feared that learning new terminology or new perspectives would alienate them from familiar social relations. Since these fears are rarely addressed as part of progressive pedagogical process, students caught in the grip of such anxiety often sit in classes feeling hostile, estranged, refusing to participate. I often face students who think that in my classes they will "naturally" not feel estranged and that part of this feeling of comfort, or being "at home," is that they will not have to work as hard as they do in other classes. These students are not expecting to find alternative pedagogy in my classes but merely "rest" from the negative tensions they may feel in the majority of other courses. It is my job to address these tensions.

If we can trust the demographics, we must assume that the academy will be full of students from diverse classes, and that more of our students than ever before will be from poor and working-class backgrounds. This change will not be reflected in the class background of professors. In my own experience, I encounter fewer and fewer academics from working-class backgrounds. Our absence is no doubt related to the way class politics and class struggle shapes who will receive graduate degrees in our society. However, constructively confronting issues of class is not simply a task for those of us who came from working-class and poor backgrounds; it is a challenge for all professors. Critiquing the way academic settings are structured to reproduce class hierarchy, Jake Ryan and Charles Sackrey emphasize "that no matter what the politics or ideological stripe of the individual professor, of what the content of his or her teaching, Marxist, anarchist, or nihilist, he or she nonetheless participates in the reproduction of the cultural and class relations of capitalism." Despite this bleak assertion they are willing to acknowledge that "nonconformist intellectuals can, through research and publication, chip away with some success at the conventional orthodoxies, nurture students with comparable ideas and intentions, or find ways to bring some fraction of the resources of the university to the service of the … class interests of the workers and others below." Any professor who commits to engaged pedagogy recognizes the importance of constructively confronting issues of class. That means welcoming the opportunity to alter our classroom practices creatively so that the democratic ideal of education for everyone can be realized.

....

If the War Goes On

Hermann Hesse provides a timely warning about the organizational and human dedication to war and security. This reading reminds us that while the doctrine of separation of powers helps keep power from accumulating in the hands of a few, the structure of government administration—bureaucracy—can take on a life of its own with a simple *modus operandi*. The efficiency of the war effort is a constant threat to democratic societies and a source of its defense.

···

from

If the War Goes On: Reflections on War and Politics

Macmillan, 1971. 22–28.[11]

Herman Hesse

Ever since I was a boy I have been in the habit of disappearing now and then, to restore myself by immersion in other worlds. My friends would look for me and after a time write me off as missing. When I finally returned, it always amused me to hear what so-called scientists had to say of my "absences," or twilight states. Though I did nothing but what was second nature to me and what sooner or later most people will be able to do, those strange beings regarded me as a kind of freak; some thought me possessed; others endowed me with miraculous powers.

So now, once again, I vanished for a time. The present had lost its charm for me after two or three years of war, and I slipped away to breathe different air. I left the plane on which we live and went to live on another plane. I spent some time in remote regions of the past, raced through nations and epochs without finding contentment, observed the usual crucifixions, intrigues, and movements of progress on earth, and then withdrew for a while into the cosmic.

When I returned, it was 1920. I was disappointed to find the nations still battling one another with the same mindless obstinacy. A few frontiers had shifted; a few choice sites of older, higher cultures had been painstakingly destroyed; but, all in all, little had changed in the outward aspect of the earth.

Great progress had been made toward equality. In Europe at least, so I heard, all countries looked the same; even the difference between belligerent and neutral countries had virtually disappeared. Since the introduction of bombing from free balloons, which automatically dropped their bombs on the civilian population from an altitude of fifty to sixty thousand feet, national boundaries, though as closely guarded as ever, had become rather illusory. The dispersion of these bombs, dropped at random from the sky, was so great that the

---

11   Hermann Hesse, "If the War Goes on Another Two Years (Early in 1918)," *If the War Goes On …*, pp. 20–28. Copyright © 1971 by Farrar, Straus and Giroux. Reprinted with permission.

balloon commands were quite content if their explosive showers had spared their own country how many landed on neutral or even allied territory had become a matter of indifference.

This was the only real progress the art of warfare had made; here at last the character of this war had found a clear expression. The world was divided into two parties which were trying to destroy each other because they both wanted the same thing, the liberation of the oppressed, the abolition of violence, and the establishment of a lasting peace. On both sides there was strong sentiment against any peace that might not last forever if eternal peace was not to be had, both parties were resolutely committed to eternal war, and the insouciance with which the military balloons rained their blessings from prodigious heights on just an unjust alike reflected the inner spirit of this war to perfection. In other respects, however, it was being waged in the old way, with enormous but inadequate resources. The meager imagination of the military men and technicians had devised a few new instruments of destruction—but the visionary who had invented the automatic bomb-strewer balloon had been the last of his kind; for in the meantime the intellectuals, visionaries, poets, and dreamers had gradually lost interest in the war, and with only soldiers and technicians to count on, the military art made little progress. With marvelous perseverance, the armies stood and lay face to face. Though, what with the shortage of metals, military decorations had long consisted exclusively of paper, no diminution of bravery had anywhere been registered.

I found my house partly destroyed by aerial bombs, but still more or less fit to sleep in. However, it was cold and uncomfortable, the rubble on the floor and the mold on the walls were distressing, and I soon went out for a walk.

A great change had come over the city; there were no shops to be seen and the streets were lifeless. Before long, a man with a tin number pinned to his hat came up to me and asked me what I was doing. I said I was taking a walk. He: Have you got a permit? I didn't understand, an altercation ensued, and he ordered me to follow him to the nearest police station.

We came to a street where all the buildings had white signs bearing the names of offices followed by numbers and letters.

One sign read: "Unoccupied civilians 2487 B 4." We went in. The usual official premises, waiting rooms and corridors smelling of paper, damp clothing, and bureaucracy. After various inquiries I was taken to Room 72 and questioned.

An official looked me over. "Can't you stand at attention?" he asked me in a stern voice. "No," I said. "Why not?" he asked. "Because I never learned how," I said timidly.

"In any case," he said, "you were taking a walk without a permit. Do you admit that?"

"Yes," I said. "That seems to be true. I didn't know. You see, I'd been ill for quite some time …"

He silenced me with a gesture. "The penalty: you are forbidden to wear shoes for three days. Take off your shoes!"

I took off my shoes.

"Good God, man!" The official was struck with horror. "Leather shoes! Where did you get them? Are you completely out of your mind?"

"I may not be quite normal mentally, I myself can't judge. I bought the shoes a few years ago."

"Don't you know that the wearing of leather shoes in any shape or form by civilians is prohibited? Your shoes are confiscated. And now let's see your identification papers!"

Merciful heavens, I had none!

"Incredible!" the official moaned. "Haven't seen anything like it in over a year!" He called in a policeman.

"Take this man to Office 19, Room 8!"

I was driven barefoot through several streets. We went into another official building, passed through corridors, breathed the smell of paper and hopelessness; then I was pushed into a room and questioned by another official. This one was in uniform.

"You were picked up on the street without identification papers. You are fined two thousand gulden. I will make out your receipt immediately."

"I beg your pardon," I faltered. "I haven't that much money on me. Couldn't you lock me up for a while instead?"

He laughed aloud.

"Lock you up? My dear fellow, what an idea! Do you expect us to feed you in the bargain? No, my friend, if you can't pay the trifling fine, I shall have to impose our heaviest penalty, temporary withdrawal of your existence permit! Kindly hand me your existence card!"

I had none.

The official was speechless. He called in two associates; they conferred in whispers, repeatedly motioning in my direction and looking at me with horror and amazement. Then my official had me led away to a detention room, pending deliberations on my case.

There several persons were sitting or standing about; a soldier stood guard at the door. I noticed that apart from my lack of shoes I was by far the best-dressed of the lot. The others treated me with a certain respect and made a seat free for me. A timid little man sidled up to me, bent down, and whispered in my ear: "I've got a magnificent bargain for you. I have a sugar beet at home. A whole sugar beet in perfect condition. It weighs almost seven pounds. Yours for the asking. What do you offer?"

He moved his ear close to my mouth, and I whispered: "You make me an offer. How much do you want?"

He whispered softly back: "Let's say a hundred and fifty gulden!"

I shook my head and looked away. Soon I was deep in thought.

I saw that I had been absent too long, it would be hard for me to adapt. I'd have given a good deal for a pair of shoes or stockings, my bare feet were miserably cold from the wet street. But everyone else in the room was barefoot too.

After a few hours they came for me. I was taken to Office 285, Room 19 f. This time the policeman stayed with me. He stationed himself between me and the official, a very high official, it seemed to me.

"You've put yourself in a very nasty position," he began. "You have been living in this city without an existence permit. You are aware no doubt that the heaviest penalties are in order."

I made a slight bow.

"If you please," I said, "I have only one request. I realize that I am quite unequal to the situation and that my position can only get worse and worse. Couldn't you condemn me to death? I should be very grateful!"

The official looked gently into my eyes.

"I understand," he said amiably. "But anybody could come asking for that! In any case, you'd need a demise card. Can you afford one? They cost four thousand gulden."

"No, I haven't got that much money. But I'd give all I have. I have an enormous desire to die."

He smiled strangely.

"I can believe that, you're not the only one. But dying isn't so simple. You belong to the state, my dear man, you are obligated to the state, body and soul. You must know that. But by the way—I see you're registered under the name of Sinclair, Emil. Could you be Sinclair, the writer?"

"That's me!"

"Oh, I'm so glad. Maybe I can do something for you. Officer, you may leave."

The policeman left the room, the official shook my hand.

"I've read your books with great interest," he said in a friendly tone, "and I'll do my best to help you.—But good God, how did you get into this incredible situation?"

"Well, you see, I was away for a while. Two or three years ago I took refuge in the cosmic, and frankly I had rather supposed the war would be over by the time I got back.—But tell me, can you get me a demise card? I'd be ever so grateful."

"It may be possible. But first you'll need an existence permit. Obviously nothing can be done without that. I'll give you a note to Office 127. On my recommendation they'll issue you a temporary existence card. But it will only be valid for two days."

"Oh, that will be more than enough!"

"Very well! When you have it, come back here to me."

We shook hands.

"One more thing," I said softly. "May I ask you a question? You must realize how little I know about what's been going on."

"Go right ahead."

"Well, here's what I'd like to know: how can life go on under these conditions? How can people stand it?"

"Oh, they're not so badly off. Your situation is exceptional: a civilian—and without papers! There are very few civilians left. Practically everyone who isn't a soldier is a civil servant. That makes life bearable for most people, a good many are genuinely happy. Little by little one gets used to the shortages. When the potatoes gave out, we had to put up with sawdust gruel—they season it with tar now, it's surprisingly tasty—we all thought it would be unbearable. But then we got used to it. And the same with everything else."

"I see," I said. "It's really not so surprising. But there's one thing I still don't understand. Tell me; why is the whole world making these enormous efforts? Putting up with such hardships, with all these laws, these thousands of bureaus and bureaucrats – what is all this meant to preserve and safeguard?"

The gentleman looked at me in amazement.

"What a question!" he cried, shaking his head. "You know we're at war; the whole world is at war. That's what we are preserving, what we make laws and endure hardships for. The war! Without these enormous exertions and achievements our armies wouldn't be able to fight for a week. They'd starve—we can't allow that!"

"Yes," I said slowly, "you've got something there! The war, in other words, is a treasure that must be preserved at any cost. Yes, but—I know it's an odd question—why do you value the war so highly? Is it worth so much? Is war really a treasure?"

The official shrugged his shoulders and gave me a pitying look. He saw that I just didn't understand.

"My dear Herr Sinclair," he said. "You've lost contact with the world. Go out into the street, talk to people; then make a slight mental effort and ask yourself: What have we got left? What is the substance of our lives? Only one answer is possible: The war is all we have left! Pleasure and personal profit, social ambition, greed, love, cultural activity—all that has gone out of existence. If there is still any law, order, or thought in the world, we have the War to thank for it.—Now do you understand?"

Yes, now I understood, and I thanked the gentleman kindly.

I left him and mechanically pocketed the recommendation to Office 127. I had no intention of using it, I had no desire to molest the gentlemen in those offices any further. Before anyone could notice me and stop me, I inwardly recited the short astral spell, turned off my heartbeat, and made my body vanish under a clump of bushes. I pursued my cosmic wanderings and abandoned the idea of going home.

....

Plessy v. Ferguson

In *Plessy v. Ferguson* the court laid out the separate but equal doctrine, which was later overturned by the holding in *Brown v. Board of Education*. Although that decision proclaimed separate will never be equal, today many jurisdictions are visibly segregated without authority of the separate but equal mentality or laws. As we work for civic change, it is important to remember the long arc of history and consider the state of mind of those who are uncomfortable with change.

....

from

Plessy v. Ferguson (No. 210)[12]

Argued: April 18, 1896; Decided: May 18, 1896

163 U.S. 537

Legislation is powerless to eradicate racial instincts or to abolish distinctions based upon physical differences, and the attempt to do so can only result in accentuating the difficulties of the present situation. If the civil and political rights of both races be equal, one cannot be inferior to the other civilly [p552] or politically. If one race be inferior to the other socially, the Constitution of the United States cannot put them upon the same plane (551–552).

543–547

By the Fourteenth Amendment, all persons born or naturalized in the United States and subject to the jurisdiction thereof are made citizens of the United States and of the State wherein they reside, and the States are forbidden from making or enforcing any law which shall abridge the privileges or immunities of citizens of the United States, or shall deprive any person of life, liberty, or property without due process of law, or deny to any person within their jurisdiction the equal protection of the laws.

The proper construction of this amendment was first called to the attention of this court in the Slaughterhouse Cases, 16 Wall. 36, which involved, however, not a question of race, but one of exclusive privileges. The case did not call for any expression of opinion as to the exact rights it was intended to secure to the colored race, but it was said generally that its main purpose was to establish the citizenship of the negro, to give definitions of citizenship of

---

12   Justice Brown, "Plessy v. Ferguson," Legal Information Institute, pp. 543–547, 551–552. Copyright in the Public Domain.

the United States and of the States, and to protect from the hostile legislation of the States the privileges and immunities of citizens of the United States, as distinguished from those of citizens of the States [p544].

The object of the amendment was undoubtedly to enforce the absolute equality of the two races before the law, but, in the nature of things, it could not have been intended to abolish distinctions based upon color, or to enforce social, as distinguished from political, equality, or a commingling of the two races upon terms unsatisfactory to either. Laws permitting, and even requiring, their separation in places where they are liable to be brought into contact do not necessarily imply the inferiority of either race to the other, and have been generally, if not universally, recognized as within the competency of the state legislatures in the exercise of their police power. The most common instance of this is connected with the establishment of separate schools for white and colored children, which has been held to be a valid exercise of the legislative power even by courts of States where the political rights of the colored race have been longest and most earnestly enforced.

One of the earliest of these cases is that of Roberts v. City of Boston, 5 Cush. 19, in which the Supreme Judicial Court of Massachusetts held that the general school committee of Boston had power to make provision for the instruction of colored children in separate schools established exclusively for them, and to prohibit their attendance upon the other schools. "The great principle," said Chief Justice Shaw, p. 206, "advanced by the learned and eloquent advocate for the plaintiff" (Mr. Charles Sumner), is that, by the constitution and laws of Massachusetts, all persons without distinction of age or sex, birth or color, origin or condition, are equal before the law. … But when this great principle comes to be applied to the actual and various conditions of persons in society, it will not warrant the assertion that men and women are legally clothed with the same civil and political powers, and that children and adults are legally to have the same functions and be subject to the same treatment, but only that the rights of all, as they are settled and regulated by law, are equally entitled to the paternal consideration and protection of the law for their maintenance and security.

Mr. Justice Bradley observed that the Fourteenth Amendment does not invest Congress with power to legislate upon subjects that are within the [p547] domain of state legislation, but to provide modes of relief against state legislation or state action of the kind referred to. It does not authorize Congress to create a code of municipal law for the regulation of private rights, but to provide modes of redress against the operation of state laws and the action of state officers, executive or judicial, when these are subversive of the fundamental rights specified in the amendment. Positive rights and privileges are undoubtedly secured by the Fourteenth Amendment, but they are secured by way of prohibition against state laws and state proceedings affecting those rights and privileges, and by power given to Congress to legislate for the purpose of carrying such prohibition into effect, and such legislation must necessarily be predicated upon such supposed state laws or state proceedings, and be directed to the correction of their operation and effect.

....

Remix

Copyright policy is a clear area where generational divide creates an uneasy criminalization of file sharing and a stifling of creativity among young digital natives. Originally protected for only a few years, and authorized under the Constitution, the monopoly of art was intended to protect individual artists and small organizations from losing the value of their efforts to create and publish their work. In the era of legal positivism, however, legislative lobbying efforts have produced copyright protection for dozens to hundreds of years for corporations and a tangled web of regulations for artists. In *Remix*, Lawrence Lessig argues for greater emphasis on creativity and the development of licenses to remix and sample. This reading shows how the power of a generation, with the aid of emerging technologies, can alter an artistic protection policy that has become heavily biased toward nonartists.

....

from

Remix: Making Art and Commerce Thrive in the Hybrid Economy

Bloomsbury, 2008. 289–294.[13]

Lawrence Lessig

Conclusion

The economic theory behind copyright justifies it as a tool to deal with what economists call the "problem of positive externalities." An "externality" is an effect that your behavior has on someone else. If you play your music very loudly and wake your neighbors, your music is producing an externality (noise). If you renovate your house and add a line of beautiful oak trees, your renovation produces an externality (beauty). Beauty is a positive externality—people generally like to receive it. Noise is a negative externality—people (especially at 3 a.m.) don't like to receive it.

Copyright law deals with the positive externality produced by the nature of creative work. Creative work is a "public good"—meaning that (1) once it is shared, anyone can consume it without reducing the amount anyone else has; and (2) it is hard to restrict anyone from consuming it once it is available to all. If you paint a beautiful mural on your garage door, my viewing it doesn't reduce your opportunity to view it. And without building a wall around your garage (not a very practical design, for a garage at least), it's very hard to block who gets to see your mural.

Jefferson put the same idea more lyrically in a letter he wrote in 1813:

> If nature has made any one thing less susceptible than all others of exclusive property, it is the action of the thinking power called an idea, which an individual may exclusively possess as long as he keeps it to himself; but the moment it is divulged, it forces itself into the possession of every one, and the receiver cannot dispossess himself of it. Its peculiar

---

13   Lawrence Lessig, "Conclusion," *Remix: Making Art and Commerce Thrive in the Hybrid Economy,* pp. 289–294. Copyright © 2008 by Penguin Books Ltd. Reprinted with permission.

character, too, is that no one possesses the less, because every other possesses the whole of it. He who receives an idea from me, receives instruction himself without lessening mine; as he who lights his taper at mine, receives light without darkening me. That ideas should freely spread from one to another over the globe, for the moral and mutual instruction of man, and improvement of his condition, seems to have been peculiarly and benevolently designed by nature, when she made them, like fire, expansible over all space, without lessening their density at any point, and like the air in which we breathe, move, and have our physical being, incapable of confinement or exclusive appropriation.

Jefferson was talking about ideas here. Copyright regulates expression. But his observations about the nature of ideas are increasingly true of expression. If I post this book on the Internet, then your taking a copy doesn't remove my having a copy too ("no one possesses the less, because every other possess the whole"). And my making a copy available for you to have makes it relatively difficult to prevent others from having a copy as well ("like the air in which we breathe, move, and have our physical being, incapable of confinement or exclusive appropriation"). "Relatively difficult," not impossible: the whole history of Digital Rights Management technology has been the aim to remake Jefferson's nature—to make it so digital objects are like physical objects (your taking one copy means one less for me; your getting access means I don't have access). But in the state of Internet nature, Internet expression is like Jefferson's ideas.

I said that economists justify copyright as a way to deal with the "problem of positive externalities." But why, you might rightly wonder, are "positive externalities" a problem? Why isn't it a positive good that expression "should freely spread from one to another over the globe, for the moral and mutual instruction of man, and improvement of his condition"? Why isn't it "peculiarly and benevolently" the Internet's "nature," to be encouraged rather than restricted?

The answer, for the economist at least, is that while free is no doubt good, if everything were free, there would be too little incentive to produce. And if there's not enough monetary incentive to produce, the economist fears, then not enough stuff is produced.

In this book I've sketched a bunch of obvious replies to this fear: there are tons of incentives beyond money. Look at the sharing economy. Look at 100 million blogs, only 13 percent of which run ads. Look at Wikipedia or Free Software. Look at academics or scientists. We have plenty of examples of creative expression produced on a model different from the one that Britney Spears employs.

But I've also made the other side to that argument clear: the sharing economy notwithstanding, there's lots that won't be created without an effective copyright regime too. I love terrible Hollywood blockbusters. If anyone could copy in high quality a Hollywood film the moment it was released, no one could afford to make $100 million blockbusters. So give me this example at least. And if there's one example, then it's plausible that there are more. Movies. Maybe music. Maybe some kinds of books—dictionaries, maybe novels by John Grisham. We should of course be skeptical about how broadly this regulation needs to reach. (Supreme Court justice Stephen Breyer got tenure at Harvard with a piece that expressed deep skepticism about how broadly this claimed need reaches.) But I'm convinced that it reaches into some places at least. For those cases, without solving the problem of positive externalities, we wouldn't have that kind of creative work.

So to get Hollywood films, some kinds of blockbuster movies, maybe Justin Timberlake-like music, and maybe a few types of books, we run a copyright system. That system is a form of regulation. Like most regulation, after a while, it becomes big and expensive. Federal courts and federal prosecutors spend a lot of money enforcing the law copyright is. Companies invest millions in technologies for protecting copyrighted material. Universities run sting operations on their own students to punish or expel those who fail to follow copyright's rule. We build this massively complex system of federal regulation—a regulation that purports to reach everyone who uses a computer—to solve this "problem" of positive externalities.

Good for us. Our government is working hard to "solve" this "problem." But what about negative externalities? What does our government do about those? Think, for example, about mercury spewed as pollution in the exhaust from coal-fired power plants. Or think about the carbon spewed from these coal-fired power plants. These too are externalities. Millions are exposed to dangerous levels of mercury because of this pollution. The planet teeters on a catastrophic climate tipping point because of this carbon. Whatever harm there might be in not having yet another *Star Trek*, the harms from these negative externalities are unquestionable and real. They cause real deaths. They will cause extraordinary dislocation and economic harm. So given its keen interest in regulating to protect against uncompensated positive externalities, what precisely has our government done about undoubtedly harmful negative externalities? In the past ten years, in a time when Congress has passed at least twenty-four copyright bills, and federal prosecutors and federal civil courts have been used to wage "war" on "piracy" so as to solve the problem of positive externalities, what exactly has the government been doing about these negative externalities?

The answer is, not much. Though President Bush successfully deflected Al Gore's charge in 2000 that we faced a carbon crisis by promising to tax carbon when elected, within two weeks of his swearing in, he reversed himself, and indicated he didn't think global warming was a problem. And though the Clean Air Act plainly regulates pollutants like mercury in power plants, in 2003, the Bush administration changed the regulations to "allow polluters to avoid actually having to reduce mercury." Thus, with these real and tangible harms caused by negative externalities, the government has done worse than nothing. At the same time, it has devoted precious resources to fighting a problem that many don't even believe is a problem at all.

So what gives?

It's been a decade since I got myself into the fight against copyright extremism. Throughout this book, I have argued that this decade's work has convinced me that this war is causing great harm to our society. Not only from losses in innovation. Not only from the stifling of certain kinds of creativity. Not only because it unjustifiably limits constitutionally guaranteed freedoms. But also, and most importantly, because it is corrupting a whole generation of our kids. We wage war against our children, and our children will become the enemy. They will become the criminals we name them to be. And because there is no good evidence to suggest that we will win this war, that's all the reason in the world to stop these hostilities—especially when there are alternatives that advance the purported governmental interest without rendering a generation criminal.

But there is insult to add to this injury. For the point is not just that our government is waging a hopeless war. It is that our government does little to fight real harm, while it wastes resources fighting "problems" that are not even clear harms.

And why does it do this?

The lesson a decade's work has taught me is that the reason has nothing to do with stupidity. It has nothing to do with ignorance. The simple reason we wage a hopeless war against our kids is that they have less money to give to political campaigns than Hollywood does. The simple reason we do nothing while our kids are poisoned with mercury, or the environment is sent over the falls with carbon, is that our kids and our environment have less money to give to campaigns than the utilities and oil companies do. Our government is fundamentally irrational for a fundamentally rational reason: policy follows not sense, but dollars.

Until that problem is solved, a whole host of problems will go unsolved. Global warming, pollution, a skewed tax system, farm subsidies: our government is irrational because it is, in an important way, corrupt. And until that corruption is solved, we should expect little good from this government.

This book is not about that corruption generally. All I have aimed for here is to get you to take one small step. Whatever you think about global warming, the environment, tax gifts to favored corporations, subsidies that benefit only corporate farmers, at least think this: there is no justification for the copyright war that we now wage against our kids. Demand that the war stop now. And once it is over, let's get on to the hard problem of crafting a copyright system that nurtures the full range of creativity and collaboration that the Internet enables: one that builds upon the economic and creative opportunity of hybrids and remix creativity; one that decriminalizes the offense of being a teen.

....

Looking for Palestine: In Reflection

We understand that identity is not a one-size-fits-all concept and that there is much fluidity between different identities we may possess. The excerpts selected from Najla Said's book, *Looking for Palestine: Growing Up Confused in an Arab-American Family*, introduce you to the challenges faced by the author as she sought to understand and bridge the various identities she held in very different environments.

....

from

Looking for Palestine: Growing Up Confused in an Arab-American Family.

Riverhead, 2013. 1–4, 51–57.[14]

Najla Said

I am a Palestinian-Lebanese-American Christian woman, but I grew up as a Jew in New York City.

I began my life, however, as a WASP.

I was born in Boston to an Ivy League literature professor and his wife, baptized into the Episcopal Church at the age of one, and, at five, sent to an all-girls private school on the Upper East Side of Manhattan, one that boasts among its alumnae such perfectly formed and well-groomed American blue bloods as the legendary Jacqueline Onassis. It was at that point that I realized that something was seriously wrong—with me.

With my green seersucker tunic, its matching bloomers (worn underneath for gym and dance classes), the white Peter Pan collar of my blouse, and my wool knee socks, I was every bit the Chapin schoolgirl. I was proud of my new green blazer with its fancy school emblem and my elegant shoes from France. But even the most elaborate uniform could not protect against my instant awareness of my differences. I was a dark-haired rat in a sea of blond perfection. I didn't live on the Upper East Side, where everyone else in my class seemed to live, but on the Upper *West* Side, or, rather, so far beyond the boundaries of what was then considered the Upper West Side as to be unacceptable to many. I did not have a canopy bed, an uncluttered bedroom, and a perfectly decorated living room the way my classmates did or like the homes I saw on TV. I had books piled high on shelves and tables, pipes, pens, Oriental rugs, painted walls, and strange houseguests. I was surrounded at home not only by some of the Western world's greatest scholars and writers—Noam Chomsky, Lillian Hellman, Norman Mailer, Jacques

---

14   Najla Said, "Looking for Palestine," *Looking for Palestine: Growing Up Confused in an Arab-American Family*, pp. 1–4, 51–57. Copyright © 2013 by Penguin Books Ltd. Reprinted with permission.

Derrida, Susan Sontag, Joan Didion—but by the creme de la creme of the Palestinian Resistance.

I know today there are probably lots of children of immigrants growing up similarly confused by the mixed messages of their lives, pertaining to everything from class to culture to standards of beauty. For me, though, growing up the daughter of a Lebanese mother and a prominent Palestinian thinker in New York City in the 1980s and '90s was confusing and unsettling. I constantly questioned everything about who I was and where I fit in the world, constantly judged my own worthiness and compared myself to others, and I struggled desperately to find a way to reconcile the beautiful, comforting, loving world of my home, culture, and family with the supposed "barbaric" and "backward" place and society others perceived it to be. I wondered why I was "an exception" to the rule of what both Arabs and Americans were "supposed" to be like, and why I was stuck in such an uneasy position.

After years of trying desperately to convince people that they didn't really understand me or the place my family came from, I stopped trying, especially since there was never anyone around to make me feel less alone in my assertions. I resigned myself to believing that everything people said about my culture was true, because it was exhausting and futile to try to convince anyone otherwise. Strangely, though, I also held on tightly to what I knew to be accurate and real about my family and culture. My parents and extended family are entirely responsible for that. I spent years simultaneously pushing them away and drawing them close, until I found a place where I could exist together with them and completely apart from them. Letting go of the idea that I had to have one identity, one way to describe myself, one "real me" hasn't left me any less confused about who I am, but it has certainly left me inspired, engaged, interested, complicated, and aware. And I'd rather be all of those things than just plain old "American," or plain old "Arab."

\- - -

That I was from the wrong side of the *global* tracks as well became clearer as the '80s began to unfold, and "Beirut" became synonymous with "war."

As a little Chapin girl in the early 1980s, it was *Lebanese* that I never wanted to be. The "Palestinian" thing never made sense. It was this funny word that my dad would use to describe himself, and I didn't even know it referred to a place. It could have been a dietary practice, a blood type, or a disease. My mother never described herself as a Palestinian, so I did not know that because Daddy was one, I was one too. Frankly, it seemed that as long as I wasn't from behind the Iron Curtain, where it was ice-cold, and where people waited in line for food and spoke like robots, I wasn't a threat. There were also very few Jewish girls in my school, and certainly no Israelis, so my lack of "Arab pride" was not completely unfounded.

And then I gradually came to learn what an Arab was and, consequently, spent a good portion of the rest of my childhood avoiding the fact that I might actually be one. It was 1979 when I began school, and the attacks of September 11 were twenty-two years away, but the words "Arab" and "Muslim" were already synonymous with "crazy, violent terrorists." Palestinians had already hijacked planes and killed Israeli athletes at the Olympics, and Lebanon was on the front page of the paper every day, engulfed in flames and fire. I was both too young to understand and hadn't been schooled in the intricacies of the Lebanese Civil War, the Israeli occupation of Palestinian lands, and the historical context of things, so when my friends made passing comments about Beirut being the most awful, dangerous place on earth, when they asserted that the Lebanese were all violent, machine-gun-wielding lunatics ("except for your family, Najla. But you're really American anyway"), and that Muslims were "weird angry" people, I couldn't really counter them with anything but a silent, sad nod.

And was I really Arab? I didn't understand how I could be. My father, the English professor, spoke Arabic sometimes with my mom and had family in Lebanon but sounded and seemed perfectly American to me. In addition, we were, as I have explained, Christian-Episcopal Baptist Presbyterian Quakers. Many of the girls I went to school with were Episcopalians, and I clung joyfully to the fact that I was a baptized Episcopalian, and dropped that piece of precious information into whatever conversation I could. For a sensitive young girl acutely aware of her differences, this one tiny similarity meant an enormous amount. So I didn't go to the church on the Upper East Side that all my friends went to (or any church for that matter). The mere fact that *I could have gone there* was enough to save me from total rejection.

"Are you Jewish or Christian?" became the question of the month at school.

"Christian," I'd say with relief. I felt terribly sad for the Jewish girls, who were in the minority, but I was mostly glad there was a new question to answer, and it was one to which I had the "right" answer.

- - -

The irony is, I probably knew more about Judaism at that point than I did about Christianity. As a family, we celebrated Christmas and Easter, but we never went to church. My grandparents were more religious than my parents, and in the very progressive time and place in which I grew up, everyone was trying to make sure that kids heard different stories and learned about the whole world. By the time I was five, I knew more African and French songs than English ones, and more about origami, Chinese New Year, and the Children of Israel than I did about myself.

During my first year of nursery school we had had a Hanukkah party one week and a Christmas party the next. At the Hanukkah party, we ate potato latkes on blue tablecloths; we heard the story of Judas Maccabeus and learned the dreidel song. Everyone got a dreidel (I still have mine), and the girls were given fans, and the boys, plastic swords. My friend Noah showed his mom his sword and told her about how "the Jewish people got to fight for their freedom." She told him he was one of those people. He was happy. I was happy for him.

My mom participated happily in Hanukkah day, as she had done for the party we had had for a Japanese holiday earlier in the year. But when she was handed a set of instructions about what was acceptable for the Christmas party, my mother spoke up. She went to my teacher and said, "Look, I don't care a *damn* about religion but if you are going to teach them all about Hanukkah and tell the story of Judas Maccabeus and oil that burned for so many days, why do you have restrictions on what we are allowed to teach them about Christmas?" She pointed to the list and read aloud: '"No angels, no Jesus, no "Hark! The Herald Angels Sing," no stars, no wise men. Reindeer, Santa Claus, bells, trees, and "Frosty the Snowman" are all okay'? How silly. If you are going to tell them one story, you should tell them the other. It's not like they won't need to learn who Jesus was at some point in their lives."

"We don't want to offend the Jewish families," my teacher said. "Well, what about the Muslim families, and the Hindu families, and the secular families? Do you want to offend *them*?"

Another mother, who was Turkish, piped up: "Yes. You know, we celebrated Ramadan not too long ago, and no one asked us if we'd like to have a party to teach the kids about it."

The next year, the teachers allowed my mother to read us a very smart children's version of the Nativity story that related the story of Jesus's birth in as unreligious a way as possible. At home, though, we never actually mentioned Jesus, much to the chagrin of Teta Hilda. My parents were adamantly secular. To me, Christmas was about presents and giving to the poor, and Easter was about chocolate bunnies and pretty dresses. But I always remember my mom's insistence that we treat everyone equally, even when it came to religion, which she abhorred.

Not only did they all belong to the "right" church, but everyone in my family also spoke English and French along with Arabic, which made us "cosmopolitan" (in my head), and my grandmother wore Chanel suits, played bridge, and visited mud baths in Czechoslovakia. I traveled to Lebanon frequently, and I ate Arabic food at home. But even though my mother spoke to me in Arabic a lot of the time, and knew only the French words for my headbands, stockings, and underwear, I had no idea she spoke with an accent until my friend Caroline told me so when we were in the fourth grade. For the most part, I was wholly unaware of the political realities of the Middle East. I didn't know what Muslims were because as far as I knew I'd never met one. Preschool had introduced me to some Jewish friends, and the candles and the dreidels, but I certainly didn't know what Israel was or what Zionism might be, and if I had known, I surely would not have been able to make a connection between those two things and a menorah.

When Teta Hilda came to kindergarten with me on Grandparents' Day, she looked just as fancy as all the other grandmas and grandpas. I knew she was not "American" in the same way that some of them were, and the way that Catherine's nana from Elizabeth, New Jersey, was, but I also did not know what an Arab was, let alone what one was "supposed to look like. Teta looked, dressed, and behaved most like the Chapin grandparents who were from France and Sweden and Italy. Her accent, like my dad's, was almost nonexistent, and sounded more fancy than foreign. Her clothes were elegant and lady-like—hardly appropriate for hanging out in a sandbox—and she was very impressed with all that was proper and genteel about Chapin. She knew by heart all the Episcopal hymns that we sang at Morning

Prayers, nodded in approval at the manners we were taught, and then took me for tea at the Stanhope Hotel, on Fifth Avenue, at the end of the day. So I assumed that Beirut was probably somewhere in Paris.

But as I grew older and progressed into the first, second, and third grades, a sense of shame about my differences—my hairy arms, my weird name, my family's missing presence on the Social Register—took over my thoughts. My grandmother's once "fancy" accent began to sound simply "foreign."

....

In reflection:

In the classroom, we prompt students to consider their identities and the groups they belong to—student, sibling, parent, team member, citizen, religious affiliations, gender, race. Do they all fit together neatly? Are there contradictions? Are there strengths in having so many identities? This is the beauty of Said's conclusion—the beauty of her confusion. She writes, "Letting go of the idea that I had to have one identity, one way to describe myself, one 'real me' hasn't left me any less confused about who I am, but it has certainly left me inspired, engaged, interested, complicated, and aware. And I'd rather be all of those things than just plain old 'American,' or plain old 'Arab.'" We hope that these pages will help you as you begin to grapple with multiple identities and how they can shape your civic identity.

Civic Development, from Identity to Advocacy through Agency, Is Democratic Education for a Diverse Twenty-First Century

We hope you have enjoyed this process of civic learning and democratic engagement. While all learners are unique and learn in their own way, we imagine a civic commons where we each can participate equally with the full confidence of our own identity and the agency to see our goals and aspirations through. As advocates we invite you to join our conversation and look forward to welcoming you into our shared civic space. Congratulations on the last step of the process, evidencing your new knowledge through your own creative expression of civic identity, agency, and advocacy!

Sotomayor: You Have to Work Harder

When we look at successful people, we may often be quick to judge or assume that their journey to success was easy and that a similar ascent to success is not available to "people like me." Supreme Court Justice Sonia Sotomayor, appointed in 2009, holds the distinction of being the first justice of Hispanic heritage, the first Latina, the court's third female justice, and its twelfth Roman Catholic justice. This history-making distinction was not handed to her—as she explains, she had to work harder, given her marginalized upbringing in the Bronx, New York, and the violence and addiction that plagued other members of her family. How did she do it? It starts early; according to Sotomayor, "each child has to have within them a desire to achieve something."

Something. That something for you can be anything—small or big. But that something starts it all. We hope that through taking this journey to understand your own civic identity, agency, and advocacy, you have found something that matters to you and something that you are willing to work for. As we mentioned at the beginning of this reader, democracy is not a spectator sport. Your community, country, and world need *you* and the unique gifts and talents you bring. Don't sell yourself short, don't say you can't possibly achieve anything. You have seen throughout history that individuals have the power to create momentous change. Who says that can't be you?

....

from

Interview: "As a Latina, Sonia Sotomayor Says, 'You Have to Work Harder,'"

National Public Radio, January 13, 2014.[1]

Sonia Sotomayor

Like most sitting Supreme Court justices, Sonia Sotomayor is circumspect when talking about the court; but she has written intimately about her personal life—more so than is customary for a Supreme Court justice.

"When I was nominated by the president for this position, it became very clear to me that many people in the public were interested in my life and the challenges I had faced," she tells Fresh Air's Terry Gross. "… And I also realized that much of the public perception of who I was and what had happened to me was not quite complete."

In her memoir, *My Beloved World*, Sotomayor recounts growing up poor in the South Bronx; living with juvenile diabetes, a chronic

---

1   "As A Latina, Sonia Sotomayor Says, 'You Have To Work Harder,'" NPR Books. Copyright © 2014 by National Public Radio (NPR). Reprinted with permission.

disease; being raised by a single mother after her father, who was an alcoholic, died; and struggling to get a good education in spite of the odds. It became a best-seller when it was published last year and has just come out in paperback.

> I watched my father, who I knew loved me, kill himself with alcohol; I watched a cousin [Nelson] whom I adored … this person who had an enormous talent and a great intelligence … destroy himself and affect his family with a great deal of pain by ultimately killing himself with drug use.
>
> That has always permitted me … as a judge … to understand that the people who came before me as defendants were human beings with good and potentially very bad things within them. It was not unusual for defendants to have families who depended on them, who loved them, who thought the world of them, even though they had done horrific things. …
>
> When I was being nominated to the [U.S.] Court of Appeals, I was asked [by] the Senate to give them a record of how often I had departed from the then-mandatory sentencing guidelines. And judges were permitted under certain circumstances to depart downward, give a lesser sentence, or depart upwards, give a higher sentence than the guidelines called for. I was shocked to find that I gave less downward departures, lesser sentences, and more greater sentences than the national average. …
>
> I think because of my experiences, however, I could treat that person in my courtroom as an individual and not as a non-entity and at the same time hold them responsible for their acts.

On how she was able to succeed while her cousin Nelson didn't, despite growing up in the same neighborhood:

> I think there's always a discussion about nature versus nurturing, but I do believe that it's always a combination of the two that impacts what happens to a person. For me, I was blessed, unlike my cousin Nelson, with being a girl. My family was more protective of me. I wasn't permitted to play outside alone. It was a different world for the boys in the family: They were permitted to go out. …
>
> I also think that each child has to have within them a desire to achieve something. For me, my initial goals were

just to graduate from college because nobody in my family had done it. But the idea of having a mark that I wanted to achieve helped me. Nelson couldn't find that in his life. He loved being a musician. Regrettably, his father wanted him to be a doctor and their dreams clashed and I think Nelson never found the support that he needed to give reality to his dreams.

On missing certain cultural references:

One day talking to my first-year roommate … I was telling her about how out of place I felt at Princeton, how I didn't connect with many of the experiences that some of my classmates were describing, and she said to me, "You're like Alice in Wonderland."

And I said, "Who is Alice?"

And she said, "You don't know about Alice?"

And I said, "No, I don't."

And she said, "It's one of the greatest book classics in English literature. You should read it."

I recognized at that moment that there were likely to be many other children's classics that I had not read. … Before I went home that summer, I asked her to give me a list of some of the books she thought were children's classics and she gave me a long list and I spent the summer reading them. That was perhaps the starkest moment of my understanding that there was a world I had missed, of things that I didn't know anything about. … [As an adult] there are moments when people make references to things that I have no idea what they're talking about.

On being Latina and her responsibility to her community:

You have to work harder. … In every position that I've been in, there have been naysayers who don't believe I'm qualified or who don't believe I can do the work. And I feel a special responsibility to prove them wrong. I think I work harder than a lot of other people because of that sense of responsibility.

Does it mean that I think that I have an obligation to any particular group including Latinos? No. My job is my job and, particularly being a judge, I would be doing a disservice to the Latino community if I ruled on the basis of a preference for any group. … I have to rule as I do on the basis of the law … but I do feel that I have a special responsibility to work harder to prove myself because I am the first of a group that has been perceived as being incapable of doing whatever it is that I've had the benefit of becoming a part of.

On women trying to "have it all":

This whole continuing question about whether women can "have it all"—I think it's the wrong question. I think the right question should be, "What makes you happy as a person? Do you want to not 'have it all' but to have both in your life in an imperfect way?" Because if the question presupposes that you're going to do both and be equally happy at every moment, it's a false question.

It's a compromise; it's a balance; it's figuring out what's the most important thing you have to give at that moment and to what. All of that is a constant work in progress.

....

In reflection:

How can you keep the dialogue going?

Inquiry Questions and Responses

We would love to see your work. Please consider sending drafts, finished products, comments, or questions to us through our website: http://imagine1civic.commons.gc.cuny.edu/.

THE LAW AND IDENTITY READER
Cultivating Understanding, Agency, and Advocacy

The Law and Identity Reader: Cultivating Understanding, Agency, and Advocacy guides readers through the development of civic understanding, beginning with individual identity. The book has been designed to encourage dialogue about what makes civic change possible and the challenges that must be overcome so that everyone can be included in this change.

The main themes of the anthology focus on active democracy, civic agency, and civic advocacy. These are examined through legal cases such as *Plessy v. Ferguson, Marbury v. Madison,* and *Brown v. The Board of Education,* seminal writings including *Federalist Paper No. 47* and Martin Luther King's *Letter from Birmingham Jail,* and readings on originalism, social class, and land reform.

Rooted in transformative learning theory and social movement research, *The Law and Identity Reader* places learners in the forefront and includes opportunities for dialogue and self-reflection. This anthology is well-suited to courses in civic engagement, law and society, governmental institutions, and democratic theory.

Jason Leggett earned his law degree, with concentrations in social justice and community development, at the Seattle University School of Law. He passed the New York Bar Exam before joining the faculty of Kingsborough Community College. His research focuses on the rule of law and cultural issues within law and society.

Helen-Margaret Nasser is the director of the Student Union and Intercultural Center at Kingsborough Community College in Brooklyn, New York. She holds a bachelor's degree from McGill University (Canada) in political science and international development studies and a master's degree in political science from the Graduate Center of the City University of New York where she concentrated on Middle East identity and civil society politics.

www.cognella.com

ISBN 978-1-5165-0914-0

90000

9 781516 509140

SKU 81810-1B-BR

cognella®
ACADEMIC PUBLISHING